The Best of Healthy
Soul Food
Recipes

Publications International, Ltd.

Dedicated to the memory of

Yolanda King
(1955–2007)

The first national Ambassador
for the American Stroke Association's
Power To End Stroke movement

American Heart Association® | American Stroke Association®
Learn and Live℠

American Heart Association Team: Linda Ball, Deborah Renza, Barthy Gaitonde, Janice Moss, Jackie Haigney, Robin Sullivan, and Eleanor Dean

Recipe Developers: Maurietta Amos, Jennifer Booker, Nancy S. Hughes, Annie King, Carol Ritchie, and Julie Shapero, R.D., L.D.

Recipe Analyst: Tammi Hancock, R.D.

Pictured on the front cover: Crab Cakes *(page 22)*.
Pictured on the back cover: Smothered Steak *(page 40)*.

ISBN-13: 978-1-4127-9652-1
ISBN-10: 1-4127-9652-0

Manufactured in U.S.A.

8 7 6 5 4 3 2 1

Microwave Cooking: Microwave ovens vary in wattage. Use the cooking times as guidelines and check for doneness before adding more time.

Recipes

You use your power every day by choosing what to eat and how to live your life. The choices you make add up to a big impact on your overall health. When you make good choices, you and your family will enjoy the benefits for years to come. The important thing is to be physically active and develop healthy eating habits. That means eating a wide variety of foods that promote good health.

Whether you are eating at home or dining out, use your power wisely and follow the recommendations below to help protect your heart:

■ Eat a variety of nutritious foods from all food groups.

- Eat a diet rich in vegetables and fruits.

- Choose whole-grain, high-fiber foods.

- Eat fish, preferably fish containing omega-3 fatty acids (for example, salmon, trout, and tuna) at least twice a week.

■ Limit foods that are high in calories but low in nutrients.

- Limit how much saturated fat, trans fat, and cholesterol you eat.

- Choose fat-free and low-fat dairy products.

- Cut back on beverages and foods with added sugars.

- Choose and prepare foods with little or no salt.

- If you drink alcohol, drink in moderation.

■ Read nutrition facts labels and ingredients lists when you shop.

For more information on the updated American Heart Association Dietary and Lifestyle Recommendations, visit **americanheart.org**.

HOW TO USE THESE RECIPES

To help you with meal planning, each recipe includes a nutrition analysis. The following guidelines give some details about how the analyses are calculated. Use the analyses to help determine how well a certain dish will fit into your overall eating plan.

- Each analysis is for a single serving; garnishes or optional ingredients are not included.

- When ingredient options are listed, the first one is analyzed. When a range of ingredients is given, the average is analyzed.

- Values for saturated, monounsaturated, and polyunsaturated fats are rounded and may not add up to the amount listed for total fat. Total fat also includes other fatty substances and glycerol.

- Processed foods can be very high in sodium. To keep the level of sodium in our recipes low, we call for unprocessed foods or low-sodium products when possible and add table salt sparingly for flavor. For instance, a recipe may use a can of no-salt-added tomatoes and a quarter-teaspoon of table salt. The amount of sodium in the finished dish will be less than if we called for a regular can of tomatoes and no table salt.

- When meat, poultry, or seafood is marinated and the marinade is discarded, we calculate only the amount of marinade absorbed.

- Analyses of meat are based on cooked lean meat with all visible fat discarded.

- We use 95% fat-free ground beef for analysis.

- When analyzing recipes that call for alcohol, we estimate that most of the alcohol calories evaporate during cooking.

- We use the abbreviations "g" for gram and "mg" for milligram.

Creamy Corn Chowder

Serves 5 ▪ *1 cup per serving*

Vegetable oil spray
1 **tablespoon light tub margarine**
½ **cup chopped onion**
½ **cup diced celery**
1¼ **cups water**
1 **small baking potato, peeled and cut into ½-inch cubes (about 1 cup)**
1 **14¾-ounce can no-salt-added cream-style corn, undrained**
1½ **cups frozen whole-kernel corn, thawed**
1 **to 2 teaspoons sugar**
1 **teaspoon salt-free powdered chicken bouillon**
¼ **teaspoon salt**
⅛ **teaspoon white pepper**
1 **cup fat-free half-and-half**
1 **tablespoon all-purpose flour**
2 **tablespoons minced fresh parsley**

Lightly spray a medium saucepan with vegetable oil spray. Melt the margarine over medium heat. Add the onion and celery. Cook for 5 minutes, or until soft but not brown, stirring occasionally. Stir in the water, potato, both corns, sugar, bouillon, salt, and pepper. Increase the heat to medium high and bring to a boil. Reduce the heat and simmer, covered, for 20 minutes, or until the potatoes are just tender, stirring occasionally.

Pour the half-and-half into a small bowl and whisk in the flour. Stir into the soup. Stir in the parsley. Simmer for 15 minutes, or until the soup has thickened, stirring frequently.

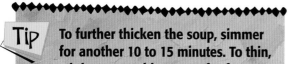

Tip To further thicken the soup, simmer for another 10 to 15 minutes. To thin, stir in 1 to 2 tablespoons fat-free half-and-half or fat-free milk.

Per Serving: Calories 184; Total Fat 1.5 g; Saturated Fat 0 g; Polyunsaturated Fat 0.5 g; Monounsaturated Fat 0.5 g; Cholesterol 0 mg; Sodium 200 mg; Carbohydrates 41 g; Dietary Fiber 3 g; Sugars 10 g; Protein 7 g

Dietary Exchanges: 2½ Starch

Soups

Chicken Soup with Mustard Greens and Tomatoes

Serves 4 ▪ *1 cup per serving*

4	cups fat-free, low-sodium chicken broth
1	small carrot, thinly sliced
4	large mustard green leaves, coarsely chopped (about 4 cups)
2	medium Italian plum tomatoes, diced
2	ounces diced lower-sodium, low-fat ham (about ¼ cup)
2	medium green onions, thinly sliced
1	tablespoon imitation bacon bits
⅛	teaspoon salt
¼	teaspoon crushed red pepper flakes

In a large saucepan, bring the broth and carrot to a simmer over medium-high heat. Reduce the heat and simmer, covered, for 5 minutes, or until the carrot is almost tender.

Stir in the remaining ingredients. Increase the heat to medium high and return to a simmer. Reduce the heat and simmer, covered, for 10 minutes, or until the greens are tender and the flavors blend. Ladle into soup bowls.

Per Serving: Calories 61, Total Fat 1.0 g, Saturated Fat 0.0 g, Polyunsaturated Fat 0.0 g, Monounsaturated Fat 0.5 g, Cholesterol 6 mg, Sodium 297 mg, Carbohydrates 7 g, Dietary Fiber 3 g, Sugars 3 g, Protein 7 g

Dietary Exchanges: 1½ Vegetable, ½ Very Lean Meat

Old-Fashioned Vegetable-Barley Soup

Serves 4 ▪ *1¼ cups per serving*

    Vegetable oil spray
  1 **teaspoon olive oil**
  ½ **medium onion, chopped**
  ½ **medium rib of celery, chopped**
  1 **medium garlic clove, minced**
  1 **14.5-ounce can no-salt-added diced tomatoes, undrained**
1½ **cups frozen mixed vegetables**
1½ **cups low-sodium vegetable broth**
  1 **cup chopped kale**
  ½ **cup water**
  ¼ **cup uncooked quick-cooking barley**
  ½ **teaspoon dried basil, crumbled**
  ½ **teaspoon dried oregano, crumbled**
  ⅛ **teaspoon pepper**
  1 **tablespoon plus 1 teaspoon shredded or grated Parmesan cheese**

Lightly spray a large Dutch oven with vegetable oil spray. Add the oil and swirl to coat the bottom. Cook the onion and celery over medium-high heat until golden, about 3 minutes, stirring occasionally. Add the garlic and cook for 10 seconds. Stir in the remaining ingredients except the Parmesan. Bring to a boil over medium-high heat. Reduce the heat and simmer, covered, for 10 to 12 minutes, or until the barley is cooked.

To serve, ladle into soup bowls and sprinkle with the Parmesan.

Per Serving: Calories 129; Total Fat 2 g; Saturated Fat 0.5 g; Polyunsaturated Fat 0.5 g; Monounsaturated Fat 1 g; Cholesterol 1 mg; Sodium 78 mg; Carbohydrates 24 g; Dietary Fiber 5 g; Sugars 5 g; Protein 6 g

Dietary Exchanges: 1 Starch, 2 Vegetable

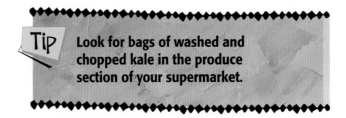

Tip Look for bags of washed and chopped kale in the produce section of your supermarket.

Variation: To make Old-Fashioned Vegetable-Barley Soup with Dumplings, prepare and cook the soup as directed on page 12, omitting the Parmesan. In a small bowl, combine ⅔ cup reduced-fat all-purpose baking mix (lowest sodium available) and 2 tablespoons finely chopped kale. Stir in ¼ cup fat-free milk until moistened.

Drop 4 mounds into the simmering soup. Simmer, covered, for an additional 15 minutes, or until a wooden toothpick or cake tester inserted into a dumpling comes out clean. (Do not remove the cover while simmering.) To serve, ladle the soup into soup bowls and top each serving with dumpling.

Per Serving: Calories 204; Total Fat 3 g; Saturated Fat 0.5 g; Polyunsaturated Fat 0.5 g; Monounsaturated Fat 1 g; Cholesterol 0 mg; Sodium 290 mg; Carbohydrates 39 g; Dietary Fiber 5 g; Sugars 7 g; Protein 7 g

Dietary Exchanges: 2 Starch, 2 Vegetable

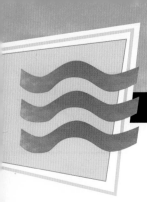

Green Bean Salad Vinaigrette

Serves 12 ▪ *½ cup per serving*

- **1 quart water for fresh green beans or ¼ cup for frozen**
- **1 pound fresh or frozen green beans**
- **1½ tablespoons raspberry vinegar or red or white wine vinegar**
- **¾ to 1 teaspoon prepared mustard**
- **½ teaspoon finely snipped fresh thyme leaves or 1½ teaspoons dried, crumbled**
- **½ teaspoon finely snipped fresh parsley or 1½ teaspoons dried, crumbled**
- **½ teaspoon honey**
- **½ medium garlic clove, minced**
- **¼ cup canola or corn oil**
- **¼ teaspoon salt**
- **⅛ teaspoon pepper, or to taste**
- **1 medium red bell pepper, cut lengthwise into thin strips**
- **½ to 1 small red onion, cut lengthwise into thin strips**
- **¼ teaspoon fresh lemon zest**

In a large saucepan, bring the water to a boil over high heat. Add the beans and boil for 5 minutes.

Meanwhile, fill a large bowl with cold water. When the beans are ready, drain them in a colander, then transfer to the cold water to stop the cooking process. Once the green beans are cold, drain well and pat dry.

While the beans are cooling, whisk together the vinegar, mustard, thyme, parsley, honey, and garlic in another large bowl. Slowly whisk in the oil, continuing to whisk until well combined. Whisk in the salt and pepper.

Add the green beans, bell pepper, and onion to the vinaigrette, tossing to coat. Cover and refrigerate for at least 30 minutes before serving. Just before serving, sprinkle with the lemon zest.

Per Serving: Calories 60; Total Fat 5 g; Saturated Fat 0.5 g; Polyunsaturated Fat 1.5 g; Monounsaturated Fat 3 g; Cholesterol 0 mg; Sodium 55 mg; Carbohydrates 4 g; Dietary Fiber 2 g; Sugars 2 g; Protein 1 g

Dietary Exchanges: 1 Vegetable

Salads

Sweet Country Coleslaw

Serves 4 ▪ *½ cup per serving*

2 **tablespoons fat-free or light sour cream**
1 **tablespoon plus 1 teaspoon sugar**
1 **tablespoon fat-free or light mayonnaise**
1 **teaspoon cider vinegar**
¼ **teaspoon celery seeds (optional)**
⅛ **teaspoon salt**
⅛ **teaspoon pepper**
4 **cups packaged shredded cabbage and carrot mix**

In a medium bowl, stir together all the ingredients except the cabbage and carrot mix. Stir in the cabbage and carrot mix until well coated. (The mixture will be very thick.) Let stand for 15 minutes before serving. (The coleslaw will shrink in volume by about half.)

Per Serving: Calories 44; Total Fat 0 g; Saturated Fat 0 g; Polyunsaturated Fat 0 g; Monounsaturated Fat 0 g; Cholesterol 2 mg; Sodium 126 mg; Carbohydrates 9 g; Dietary Fiber 1 g; Sugars 7 g; Protein 1 g

Dietary Exchanges: ½ Other Carbohydrate

Potato Salad

Serves 4 ▪ *½ cup per serving*

2	cups water
10	ounces red potatoes, peeled and cut into ½-inch cubes
½	medium rib of celery, finely chopped
⅓	cup finely chopped yellow or white onion (about 1 small) or green onions (about 3 medium, green and white parts)
2	tablespoons fat-free or light mayonnaise
2	tablespoons fat-free or light sour cream
2 to 3	teaspoons sweet pickle relish
½	teaspoon prepared mustard
¼	teaspoon salt
⅛	teaspoon pepper

In a medium saucepan, bring the water to a boil over high heat. Add the potatoes and return to a boil. Reduce the heat and simmer, covered, for 4 to 5 minutes, or until the potatoes are just tender. Drain in a colander. Run the potatoes under cold water for about 20 seconds to stop the cooking process. Drain well in a colander.

In a medium bowl, stir together the remaining ingredients. Using a rubber scraper, gently fold the potatoes into the mixture. Cover and refrigerate for 2 to 3 hours. The flavor and texture are at their peak if the salad is served the day it is made.

Per Serving: Calories 70; Total Fat 0.5 g; Saturated Fat 0 g; Polyunsaturated Fat 0 g; Monounsaturated Fat 0 g; Cholesterol 2 mg; Sodium 251 mg; Carbohydrates 14 g; Dietary Fiber 2 g; Sugars 3 g; Protein 2 g

Dietary Exchanges: 1 Starch

Macaroni Salad

Serves 6 ▪ *½ cup per serving*

4 ounces dried elbow macaroni
¼ cup finely chopped green onions
¼ cup fat-free or light sour cream
3 tablespoons fat-free or light mayonnaise
2 tablespoons sweet pickle relish
1 teaspoon spicy brown mustard (lowest sodium available)
⅓ cup chopped seeded cucumber
⅓ cup chopped celery
⅓ cup chopped red bell pepper
¼ cup grated carrot

In a medium saucepan, prepare the pasta using the package directions, omitting the salt and oil. Pour into a colander and rinse under cold water. Drain well.

In a medium bowl, stir together the green onions, sour cream, mayonnaise, pickle relish, and mustard. Using a rubber scraper, gently fold in the pasta and remaining ingredients. Cover and refrigerate for 1 to 2 hours, or until well chilled, before serving.

Per Serving: Calories 101, Total Fat 0.5 g, Saturated Fat 0.0 g, Polyunsaturated Fat 0.0 g, Monounsaturated Fat 0.0 g, Cholesterol 3 mg, Sodium 138 mg, Carbohydrates 20 g, Dietary Fiber 2 g, Sugars 3 g, Protein 3 g

Dietary Exchanges: 1½ Starch

Carrot-Pineapple Salad with Golden Raisins

Serves 6 ▪ *½ cup per serving*

2½ cups matchstick-size carrot strips

1 8-ounce can pineapple tidbits in their own juice, drained, reserving 1 tablespoon juice

⅓ cup golden raisins

2 tablespoons sugar

2 tablespoons light mayonnaise

½ teaspoon curry powder (optional)

In a medium bowl, stir together the carrots, pineapple, and raisins.

In a small bowl, stir together the reserved pineapple juice, sugar, mayonnaise, and curry powder. Pour over the carrot mixture. Stir gently to coat. Spoon into a serving bowl.

Per Serving: Calories 99, Total Fat 2.0 g, Saturated Fat 0.0 g, Polyunsaturated Fat 0.5 g, Monounsaturated Fat 1.0 g, Cholesterol 2 mg, Sodium 81 mg, Carbohydrates 22 g, Dietary Fiber 2 g, Sugars 16 g, Protein 1 g

Dietary Exchanges: 1 Fruit, 1½ Vegetable, ½ Fat

Tip — Even if you think you don't like curry powder, you may want to give it a try in this recipe. The curry powder is subtle, yet really brings the flavors together.

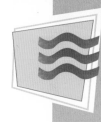

Apricot Waldorf Salad

Serves 4 ▪ *½ cup per serving*

1 medium sweet-tart apple, such as Gala, Fuji, or Granny Smith, diced (leave peel on)

1 medium rib of celery, diced

2 tablespoons coarsely chopped walnuts, dry roasted

2 tablespoons diced dried apricots

2 tablespoons fat-free or light mayonnaise

1 teaspoon fresh lemon juice

⅛ teaspoon almond extract

4 Bibb lettuce leaves

In a medium bowl, stir together the apple, celery, walnuts, and apricots. Add the mayonnaise, lemon juice, and almond extract, stirring thoroughly to coat all the ingredients. To serve, place a lettuce leaf on each salad plate. Spoon ½ cup salad onto each leaf.

Per Serving: Calories 61, Total Fat 3.0 g, Saturated Fat 0.5 g, Polyunsaturated Fat 2.0 g, Monounsaturated Fat 0.5 g, Cholesterol 1 mg, Sodium 69 mg, Carbohydrates 9 g, Dietary Fiber 2 g, Sugars 7 g, Protein 1 g

Dietary Exchanges: ½ Fruit, ½ Fat

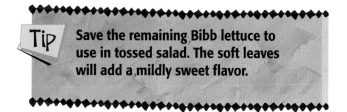

Tip Save the remaining Bibb lettuce to use in tossed salad. The soft leaves will add a mildly sweet flavor.

Crab Cakes

Serves 4 ▪ *2 crab cakes and 1 tablespoon sauce per serving*

1	6-ounce can lump crabmeat, drained
½	cup shredded carrots
¼	cup plain dry bread crumbs
2	medium green onions, thinly sliced
	Whites of 2 large eggs, lightly beaten
1	tablespoon fat-free or light mayonnaise
1	teaspoon salt-free Cajun or Creole seasoning blend *(see tip on page 68)*
¼	cup plain dry bread crumbs
2	teaspoons olive oil
3	tablespoons fat-free or low-fat sour cream
1	tablespoon fat-free or light mayonnaise
2	teaspoons fresh lemon juice
2	teaspoons bottled white horseradish
⅛	teaspoon paprika (optional)

In a medium bowl, stir together the crabmeat, carrots, ¼ cup bread crumbs, green onions, egg whites, 1 tablespoon mayonnaise, and seasoning blend.

To shape the crab cakes easily, spread the remaining ¼ cup bread crumbs on a dinner plate. Place a 2-inch round cookie cutter or biscuit cutter on the plate. Spoon about 2 tablespoons crab mixture into the cookie cutter. Using a spoon, gently press the mixture down into the cutter. Sprinkle a small amount of the bread crumbs on top of the crab mixture. Carefully remove the cutter and place it on a different space on the plate. Repeat with the remaining crab mixture and bread crumbs until you have 8 crab cakes.

Heat the oil in a large nonstick skillet over medium heat, swirling to coat the bottom. Cook the crab cakes for 2 to 3 minutes on each side, or until they are golden brown and cooked through.

Meanwhile, in a small bowl, stir together the remaining ingredients except the paprika.

To serve, put 2 crab cakes on each plate. Spoon 1½ teaspoons sauce over each crab cake. Sprinkle with the paprika.

Per Serving: Calories 151, Total Fat 4.0 g, Saturated Fat 0.5 g, Polyunsaturated Fat 0.5 g, Monounsaturated Fat 2.0 g, Cholesterol 33 mg, Sodium 371 mg, Carbohydrates 16 g, Dietary Fiber 2 g, Sugars 4 g, Protein 14 g

Dietary Exchanges: 1 Starch, 1½ Lean Meat

Seafood

Blackened Tilapia

Serves 4 ▪ *3 ounces fish per serving*

4 tilapia fillets (about 4 ounces each)
2 teaspoons paprika
1 teaspoon dried oregano, crumbled
1 teaspoon chili powder
¼ teaspoon salt
¼ teaspoon pepper
⅛ teaspoon cayenne
2 teaspoons olive oil
1 medium lemon, quartered (optional)

Rinse the fish and pat dry with paper towels.

In a small bowl, stir together the paprika, oregano, chili powder, salt, pepper, and cayenne. Sprinkle over both sides of the fish. Using your fingertips, gently press the mixture into the fish so it will adhere.

Heat a large nonstick skillet over medium-high heat. Add the oil and swirl to coat the bottom. Cook the fish for 2 minutes. Turn and cook for 2 to 3 minutes, or until the fish flakes easily when tested with a fork.

Serve with the lemon wedges.

Per Serving: Calories 136; Total Fat 4.5 g; Saturated Fat 1 g; Polyunsaturated Fat 1 g; Monounsaturated Fat 2 g; Cholesterol 57 mg; Sodium 205 mg; Carbohydrates 1 g; Dietary Fiber 1 g; Sugars 0 g; Protein 23 g

Dietary Exchanges: 3 Lean Meat

Tuna Noodle Supper

Serves 4 ▪ *1½ cups per serving*

- **2** **cups dried whole-wheat rotini (about 6 ounces)**
- **¼** **cup plain dry bread crumbs**
- **2** **tablespoons sliced almonds**
- **2** **teaspoons olive oil**
- **1** **pound sliced button or baby portobello mushrooms, or a combination**
- **1** **cup fat-free milk**
- **1** **cup fat-free, low-sodium chicken broth**
- **2** **tablespoons all-purpose flour**
- **¼** **teaspoon salt**
- **¼** **teaspoon pepper**
- **1** **12-ounce can tuna in distilled or spring water, rinsed, drained, and flaked**
- **¼** **cup shredded or grated Parmesan cheese**

Prepare the pasta using the package directions, omitting the salt and oil. Drain well in a colander. Set aside.

Meanwhile, in a large nonstick skillet, cook the bread crumbs and nuts over medium-high heat for 1 minute, or until just beginning to brown, stirring constantly. Transfer to a small plate.

In the same skillet, heat the oil over medium-high heat, swirling to coat the bottom. Cook the mushrooms for 5 to 6 minutes, or until tender, stirring occasionally.

In a small bowl, whisk together the milk, broth, flour, salt, and pepper. Pour into the mushrooms, stirring to combine. Bring to a simmer. Cook for 2 to 3 minutes, or until thickened, stirring occasionally. Stir in the tuna and Parmesan. Cook for 2 minutes, or until warmed through, stirring occasionally. Stir in the pasta. Cook for 1 minute, or until warmed through, stirring occasionally. Sprinkle with the bread crumbs and almonds. Spoon onto plates.

Per Serving: Calories 404, Total Fat 9.0 g, Saturated Fat 2.5 g, Polyunsaturated Fat 2.0 g, Monounsaturated Fat 4.0 g, Cholesterol 41 mg, Sodium 410 mg, Carbohydrates 47 g, Dietary Fiber 7 g, Sugars 7 g, Protein 36 g

Dietary Exchanges: 3 Starch, 4 Lean Meat

Shrimp Gumbo

Serves 6 ▪ *1 cup gumbo and ⅓ cup rice per serving*

2	tablespoons all-purpose flour
2	teaspoons olive oil
1	medium onion, chopped
1	medium green bell pepper, chopped
1	to 1½ medium ribs of celery, sliced
1	14.5-ounce can no-salt-added diced tomatoes, undrained
10	ounces frozen sliced okra, thawed (about 2 cups)
10½	ounces canned fat-free, low-sodium chicken broth
2	bay leaves
1	tablespoon Worcestershire sauce (lowest sodium available)
1	teaspoon sugar
¾	teaspoon dried thyme, crumbled
4	ounces canned fat-free, low-sodium chicken broth
1	pound fresh or frozen peeled raw medium shrimp, thawed if frozen
1	tablespoon olive oil
¾	teaspoon salt
¼	teaspoon red hot-pepper sauce
1	cup uncooked instant brown or white rice

Heat a Dutch oven over medium heat. Cook the flour for 1 to 1½ minutes, or until beginning to turn off-white, stirring constantly. Do not overcook. Transfer to a plate.

Add 2 teaspoons oil to the pot and swirl to coat the bottom. Cook the onion, bell pepper, and celery for 5 minutes, stirring frequently. Stir in the undrained tomatoes, okra, 10½ ounces broth, bay leaves, Worcestershire sauce, sugar, and thyme.

In a jar with a tight-fitting lid, combine the remaining broth and the reserved flour. Cover and shake until completely blended. Stir into the tomato mixture. Bring to a boil over high heat. Reduce the heat and simmer, covered, for 25 minutes, or until the okra is very tender and the mixture has thickened, stirring frequently.

Stir in the shrimp. Cook, covered, for 5 minutes, or until the shrimp turn pink. Remove from the heat.

Stir in 1 tablespoon oil, salt, and hot-pepper sauce. Let stand for at least 15 minutes. Discard the bay leaves.

Meanwhile, prepare the rice using the package directions, omitting the salt and margarine.

To serve, spoon the rice into soup bowls. Ladle the gumbo over the rice.

Per Serving: Calories 205; Total Fat 5 g; Saturated Fat 0.5 g; Polyunsaturated Fat 1 g; Monounsaturated Fat 3 g; Cholesterol 112 mg; Sodium 461 mg; Carbohydrates 24 g; Dietary Fiber 4 g; Sugars 6 g; Protein 16 g

Dietary Exchanges: 1 Starch, 2 Vegetable, 2 Lean Meat

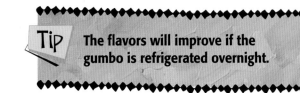

Tip **The flavors will improve if the gumbo is refrigerated overnight.**

Oven–Fried Catfish with Tartar Sauce

Serves 4 ▪ *3 ounces fish and 1 tablespoon sauce per serving*

Vegetable oil spray
- ⅓ **cup yellow cornmeal**
- 2 **tablespoons all-purpose flour**
- 1 **teaspoon salt-free extra-spicy seasoning blend**
- 1 **teaspoon paprika**
- ½ **teaspoon onion powder**
- ½ **teaspoon garlic powder**
- ¼ **teaspoon salt**
- ¼ **teaspoon pepper**
- ¼ **cup fat-free or low-fat buttermilk**
- 1 **teaspoon fresh lemon juice**
- 4 **catfish fillets (about 4 ounces each)**
- 3 **tablespoons fat-free or light mayonnaise**
- 2 **tablespoons sweet pickle relish**
- 2 **teaspoons fresh lemon juice**
- ½ **teaspoon red hot-pepper sauce**
- ¼ **teaspoon sugar**
- 1 **medium lemon, quartered (optional)**

Preheat the oven to 450°F. Lightly spray a baking sheet with vegetable oil spray.

In a shallow bowl, stir together the cornmeal, flour, seasoning blend, paprika, onion powder, garlic powder, salt, and pepper.

In a large shallow bowl, stir together the buttermilk and 1 teaspoon lemon juice. Set the bowl beside the cornmeal mixture.

Rinse the fish and pat dry. Dip each fish fillet in the buttermilk mixture, turning to coat. Dredge in the cornmeal mixture, covering completely. Place on the baking sheet. Lightly spray the top of the fish with vegetable oil spray. Bake for 15 minutes, or until the fish is golden brown and flakes easily when tested with a fork.

In a small bowl, stir together the mayonnaise, relish, 2 teaspoons lemon juice, pepper sauce, and sugar. Spoon the sauce over the fish and garnish with the lemon.

Per Serving: Calories 194; Total Fat 4 g; Saturated Fat 1 g; Polyunsaturated Fat 1 g; Monounsaturated Fat 1 g; Cholesterol 68 mg; Sodium 367 mg; Carbohydrates 19 g; Dietary Fiber 1 g; Sugars 4 g; Protein 21 g

Dietary Exchanges: 1½ Starch, 3 Very Lean Meat

Sweet Spiced Salmon

Serves 4 ▪ *3 ounces fish per serving*

½ tablespoon grated orange zest
¼ cup fresh orange juice
2 tablespoons fresh lemon juice
4 salmon fillets with skin (about 5 ounces each)
1½ tablespoons firmly packed dark brown sugar
½ teaspoon paprika
½ teaspoon curry powder
½ teaspoon salt
¼ teaspoon ground cinnamon
⅛ teaspoon cayenne
  Vegetable oil spray
1 medium lemon, quartered (optional)

Set the orange zest aside in a small bowl.

In a large resealable plastic bag, combine the orange juice and lemon juice. Rinse the salmon and pat dry with paper towels. Add to the juice mixture. Seal the bag. Turn several times to coat evenly. Refrigerate for 30 minutes, turning occasionally.

Meanwhile, stir the brown sugar, paprika, curry powder, salt, cinnamon, and cayenne into the orange zest. Set aside.

Preheat the oven to 425°F. Line a baking sheet with aluminum foil. Lightly spray the foil with vegetable oil spray.

Remove the salmon from the marinade. Discard the marinade. Arrange the salmon with the skin side down on the baking sheet. Rub the brown sugar mixture over the salmon.

Bake for 14 minutes, or until the salmon flakes easily when tested with a fork.

To serve, use a metal spatula to lift the salmon flesh from the skin. Place the salmon on plates. Serve with the lemon wedges to squeeze over the salmon.

Per Serving: Calories 187; Total Fat 5 g; Saturated Fat 1 g; Polyunsaturated Fat 2 g; Monounsaturated Fat 1.5 g; Cholesterol 74 mg; Sodium 388 mg; Carbohydrates 6 g; Dietary Fiber 0 g; Sugars 5 g; Protein 28 g

Dietary Exchanges: ½ Other Carbohydrate, 4 Very Lean Meat

 **Tip** Marinate the salmon for only 30 minutes so the texture will remain firm.

Spicy Oven-Fried Chicken

Serves 4 ▪ *3 ounces chicken per serving*

Vegetable oil spray
¼ **cup fat-free or low-fat buttermilk**
¼ **cup cornflake crumbs**
¼ **cup yellow cornmeal**
2 **tablespoons all-purpose flour**
1 **teaspoon salt-free extra-spicy seasoning blend**
1 **teaspoon garlic powder**
½ **teaspoon paprika**
¼ **teaspoon cayenne**
¼ **teaspoon salt**
⅛ **teaspoon dry mustard**
4 **boneless, skinless chicken breast halves (about 4 ounces each),
  all visible fat discarded**

Preheat the oven to 375°F. Lightly spray an 8- or 9-inch square baking pan or a baking sheet with vegetable oil spray.

Pour the buttermilk into a pie pan or shallow bowl.

In a large airtight plastic bag, combine the remaining ingredients except the chicken.

Set the pie pan, plastic bag, and baking pan in a row, assembly-line fashion. Put a piece of chicken in the buttermilk and turn to cover completely. Put the chicken in the plastic bag and shake to coat. Place the chicken in the baking pan. Repeat with the remaining chicken. Lightly spray the tops of the chicken with vegetable oil spray. Bake for 30 minutes, or until the chicken is no longer pink in the center and the coating is crisp.

Per Serving: Calories 195; Total Fat 1.5 g; Saturated Fat 0.5 g; Polyunsaturated Fat 0.5 g; Monounsaturated Fat 0.5 g; Cholesterol 66 mg; Sodium 264 mg; Carbohydrates 16 g; Dietary Fiber 1 g; Sugars 1 g; Protein 28 g

Dietary Exchanges: 1 Starch, 3 Very Lean Meat

Poultry

Hoppin' John

Serves 4 ▪ *1 cup per serving*

½   cup uncooked instant brown or white rice

1   teaspoon canola or corn oil

3   ounces low-fat smoked turkey sausage ring (lowest fat and sodium available), quartered lengthwise and cut into ¼-inch pieces

½   medium red bell pepper, finely chopped

1   medium jalapeño, seeded and finely chopped (wear plastic gloves when handling)

1   15-ounce can no-salt-added black-eyed peas, rinsed and drained

½   cup water

¼   teaspoon salt

Prepare the rice using the package directions, omitting the salt and margarine.

Meanwhile, in a medium nonstick skillet, heat the oil over medium-high heat, swirling to coat the bottom. Cook the sausage for 3 minutes, or until richly browned, stirring frequently. Stir in the bell pepper and jalapeño. Cook for 1 minute. Stir in the peas, water, and salt. Cook for 2 minutes, or until the mixture is thickened slightly but some liquid remains. Remove from the heat.

Let stand, covered, for 5 minutes so the flavors blend. Stir in the rice. Transfer to a serving bowl.

Per Serving: Calories 182, Total Fat 4.0 g, Saturated Fat 1.0 g, Polyunsaturated Fat 1.0 g, Monounsaturated Fat 2.0 g, Cholesterol 14 mg, Sodium 350 mg, Carbohydrates 27 g, Dietary Fiber 5 g, Sugars 5 g, Protein 10 g

Dietary Exchanges: 2 Starch, 1 Very Lean Meat

Sweet and Spicy Barbecue Chicken

Serves 4 ▪ *3 ounces chicken per serving*

> 4 skinless chicken breast halves with bone (about 6 ounces each), all visible fat discarded
> ¼ teaspoon garlic powder
> ⅛ teaspoon pepper

Sauce

> ⅓ cup no-salt-added ketchup
> ¼ cup firmly packed dark brown sugar
> 2 tablespoons cider vinegar
> 2 tablespoons honey
> 1 tablespoon Worcestershire sauce (lowest sodium available)
> ½ teaspoon salt
> ¼ teaspoon ground allspice
> ⅛ teaspoon cayenne (optional)

Preheat the broiler. Line the broiler pan with aluminum foil.

Sprinkle the chicken with the garlic powder and pepper. Broil the chicken about 4 inches from the heat for 12 minutes, or until slightly pink in the center, turning every 4 minutes. (The chicken will not be totally cooked at this point.)

Meanwhile, in a small saucepan, stir together the sauce ingredients. Bring to a boil over medium-high heat. Reduce the heat and simmer for 5 minutes, or until reduced to about ½ cup, stirring frequently. Remove from the heat. Put 2 tablespoons sauce in a small bowl, leaving the remaining sauce in the pan.

After 12 minutes, turn the chicken and brush with half the sauce in the pan. Broil for 2 minutes. Turn the chicken. Brush with the remaining sauce in the pan. Broil for 1 minute, or until the chicken is just beginning to brown and is no longer pink in the center.

To serve, put the chicken with the smooth side up on plates. Brush with the reserved 2 tablespoons sauce.

Per Serving: Calories 289; Total Fat 2 g; Saturated Fat 0.5 g; Polyunsaturated Fat 0.5 g; Monounsaturated Fat 0.5 g; Cholesterol 99 mg; Sodium 419 mg; Carbohydrates 27 g; Dietary Fiber 0 g; Sugars 25 g; Protein 39 g

Dietary Exchanges: 2 Other Carbohydrate, 5 Very Lean Meat

Baked Turkey Wings

Serves 4 ▪ *3 ounces turkey per serving*

½ **teaspoon garlic powder**
½ **teaspoon onion powder**
½ **teaspoon paprika**
½ **teaspoon salt**
¼ **teaspoon poultry seasoning**
¼ **teaspoon pepper**
1 **teaspoon olive oil**
2 **turkey wings with skin (about 3 pounds), all visible fat discarded**
4 **medium ribs of celery, quartered**

Preheat the oven to 350°F. Line a baking sheet with aluminum foil.

In a small bowl, stir together the garlic powder, onion powder, paprika, salt, poultry seasoning, and pepper.

Drizzle the oil over the turkey wings. Sprinkle with the garlic powder mixture.

Arrange the celery on the baking sheet so it will be a rack to keep the turkey from sitting in the grease. (It will also add flavor to the turkey.) Place the turkey on the celery.

Bake for 50 to 55 minutes, or until an instant-read thermometer reaches 165°F when inserted in the thickest part of the wing.

Discard the celery and the skin and all visible fat from the wings. Slice the turkey from the bone before serving.

Per Serving: Calories 185; Total Fat 4.5 g; Saturated Fat 1.5 g; Polyunsaturated Fat 1 g; Monounsaturated Fat 1.5 g; Cholesterol 104 mg; Sodium 403 mg; Carbohydrates 2 g; Dietary Fiber 1 g; Sugars 1 g; Protein 32 g

Dietary Exchanges: 4 Very Lean Meat

Chicken and Dumplings

Serves 4 ▪ *1½ cups and 7 dumplings per serving*

1 chicken breast with bone, 1 chicken thigh, and 1 chicken leg (about 2½ pounds), skin and all visible fat discarded
4 cups water
2 cups fat-free, low-sodium chicken broth
⅛ teaspoon pepper
1 cup all-purpose flour
½ teaspoon salt-free all-purpose seasoning
¼ teaspoon baking soda
1½ tablespoons light tub margarine
⅓ cup fat-free or low-fat buttermilk (plus more as needed)
All-purpose flour for dusting
1 large carrot, chopped
2 medium ribs of celery, chopped
½ medium onion, chopped
Fresh parsley, finely snipped (optional)

In a large saucepan, combine the chicken, water, broth, and pepper. Bring to a simmer over medium-high heat. Reduce the heat and simmer, covered, for 45 to 50 minutes, or until the chicken is cooked through. Using a slotted spoon, transfer the chicken to a cutting board. Turn the heat off, leaving the pan of liquid on the burner. Let the chicken cool for 15 to 20 minutes, or until easy to handle. Remove from the bones. Cut the chicken into bite-size pieces.

Meanwhile, in a medium bowl, whisk together the 1 cup flour, all-purpose seasoning, and baking soda. Using a pastry blender or fork, cut in the margarine until the margarine pieces are about pea size. Stir in the buttermilk until the dough is just moistened. (Do not overmix or the dumplings will be tough.) If the mixture is too dry, add buttermilk, 1 tablespoon at a time, until the dough holds together.

Lightly sprinkle a flat work surface with the flour for dusting. Put the dough on the work surface. Knead lightly three or four times so the dough holds together in a ball and is very slightly elastic. With floured hands or a floured rolling pin, pat or roll the dough to ¼-inch thickness. With a knife or pizza cutter, cut the dough into 28 pieces, each about 2 inches long by 1 inch wide. Cover with a dry towel.

Return the chicken to the pan. Stir in the carrot, celery, and onion. Bring to a simmer over medium-high heat. Reduce the heat and simmer, covered, for 10 minutes, or until the vegetables are tender.

Stir in the dumplings. Reduce the heat and simmer, uncovered, stirring occasionally, for 6 to 8 minutes, or until the dumplings are cooked through and the cooking liquid has thickened. (Dumplings should be opaque in the center and not taste raw.) Garnish with parsley, if desired.

Per Serving: Calories 320; Total Fat 6 g; Saturated Fat 1 g; Polyunsaturated Fat 1.5 g; Monounsaturated Fat 2 g; Cholesterol 95 mg; Sodium 307 mg; Carbohydrates 29 g; Dietary Fiber 2 g; Sugars 3 g; Protein 35 g

Dietary Exchanges: 1½ Starch, 1 Vegetable, 4 Very Lean Meat

Tip

Time-Saver: Use 2 cups chopped cooked skinless chicken (cooked without salt) for the uncooked chicken, omit the water and pepper, and increase the broth to 6 cups. Add the vegetables as directed and continue with the rest of the recipe.

Chicken Jambalaya

Serves 4 ▪ *1½ cups per serving*

Vegetable oil spray

  4 ounces low-fat smoked sausage (lowest fat and sodium available), cut into bite-size pieces

  1 medium onion, chopped

12 ounces boneless, skinless chicken breasts, all visible fat discarded, cut into bite-size pieces

  ½ medium red bell pepper, chopped

  ½ medium green bell pepper, chopped

  ¾ cup uncooked long-grain rice

  3 medium garlic cloves, minced

  1 teaspoon salt-free extra-spicy seasoning blend

  ½ teaspoon dried thyme, crumbled

  ½ teaspoon dried oregano, crumbled

  1 14.5-ounce can no-salt-added diced tomatoes, undrained

  ¾ cup fat-free, low-sodium chicken broth

    Red hot-pepper sauce (optional)

Lightly spray a Dutch oven with vegetable oil spray. Heat over medium-high heat. Cook the sausage and onion for 2 to 3 minutes, or until the onion is soft, stirring constantly. Stir in the chicken and bell peppers. Cook for 4 minutes, or until the chicken is no longer pink on the outside, stirring frequently. Reduce the heat to medium low. Stir in the rice, garlic, seasoning blend, thyme, and oregano. Cook for 2 minutes, stirring frequently. Stir in the undrained tomatoes and broth. Increase the heat to high and bring to a boil. Reduce the heat and simmer, covered, for 20 minutes, or until the rice is thoroughly cooked.

Ladle into bowls. Serve with the hot-pepper sauce.

Per Serving: Calories 302, Total Fat 4.0 g, Saturated Fat 1.0 g, Polyunsaturated Fat 1.0 g, Monounsaturated Fat 1.5 g, Cholesterol 68 mg, Sodium 378 mg, Carbohydrates 38 g, Dietary Fiber 3 g, Sugars 7 g, Protein 28 g

Dietary Exchanges: 2 Starch, 1½ Vegetable, 3 Very Lean Meat

Smothered Steak

Serves 4 ▪ *3 ounces steak and ½ cup vegetables per serving*

2   tablespoons all-purpose flour
¼   teaspoon pepper
4   eye-of-round steaks (about 4 ounces each), all visible fat discarded
2   teaspoons canola or corn oil
8   ounces sliced button mushrooms
½   medium onion, thinly sliced
1   cup fat-free, no-salt-added beef broth
2   tablespoons imitation bacon bits
2   teaspoons soy sauce (lowest sodium available)
1   teaspoon molasses
1   cup frozen green beans

In a shallow bowl or plate, stir together the flour and pepper. Coat the steaks on both sides with the mixture, shaking off the excess.

Heat a large nonstick skillet over medium-high heat. Add the oil and swirl to coat the bottom. Cook the steaks for 2 to 3 minutes on each side, or until browned. Transfer to a plate.

In the same skillet, cook the mushrooms and onion for 2 to 3 minutes, or until the onion is tender-crisp, scraping to dislodge any browned bits and stirring occasionally. Stir in the broth, bacon bits, soy sauce, and molasses. Add the steaks. Bring to a simmer, still on medium high. Reduce the heat and simmer, covered, for 35 to 40 minutes, or until the steaks are almost tender. Stir in the green beans. Simmer for 6 to 8 minutes, or until the steaks are tender and the beans are cooked through.

Slow-Cooker Method: After browning the steaks and cooking the mushrooms and onion, put all the ingredients except the green beans in a slow cooker. Cook on low for 4 to 6 hours, adding the green beans for the last hour of cooking, or on high for 2 to 3 hours, adding the green beans for the last 30 minutes of cooking.

Per Serving: Calories 222; Total Fat 6.5 g; Saturated Fat 1.5 g; Polyunsaturated Fat 1 g; Monounsaturated Fat 3 g; Cholesterol 47 mg; Sodium 172 mg; Carbohydrates 11 g; Dietary Fiber 2 g; Sugars 3 g; Protein 30 g

Dietary Exchanges: ½ Starch, 1 Vegetable, 3 Lean Meat

Meats

Garlic Pork Roast

Serves 8 ▪ 3 ounces pork and 2 tablespoons onion mixture per serving

Vegetable oil spray

1 **2-pound boneless top loin pork roast (not tenderloin), all visible fat discarded**
4 **medium garlic cloves, halved lengthwise**
½ **teaspoon pepper (coarsely ground preferred)**
½ **teaspoon paprika**
2 **teaspoons olive oil, divided use**
3 **medium onions (about 12 ounces), thinly sliced**
¼ **teaspoon salt**
¼ **cup water**
¼ **teaspoon salt**

Preheat the oven to 325°F. Lightly spray an 11×7×2-inch baking pan with vegetable oil spray.

Using a paring knife, make 8 small, widely spaced slits in the pork. Place half a garlic clove in each. Sprinkle the pepper and paprika over the pork. Using your fingertips, gently press the pepper and paprika so they adhere to the pork.

In a large nonstick skillet, heat 1 teaspoon oil over medium-high heat, swirling to coat the bottom. Cook the pork for 2 minutes on each side, or until richly browned. Transfer to the baking pan. Set aside.

In the same skillet, heat the remaining 1 teaspoon oil over medium-high heat, swirling to coat the bottom. Scrape to dislodge any browned bits. Cook the onions and ¼ teaspoon salt for 7 minutes, or until the onions are richly browned, stirring frequently. Pour the water into the skillet. Stir. Spoon the mixture around the pork in the baking pan. Sprinkle the pork with the remaining salt.

Bake, covered, for 1 hour 15 minutes, or until the internal temperature registers 155°F on a meat or instant-read thermometer. Transfer the pork to a cutting board. Let stand for 10 minutes so the pork will continue to cook. Slice. Serve with the onion mixture.

Per Serving: Calories 163, Total Fat 5.0 g, Saturated Fat 1.5 g, Polyunsaturated Fat 0.5 g, Monounsaturated Fat 2.5 g, Cholesterol 56 mg, Sodium 289 mg, Carbohydrates 6 g, Dietary Fiber 1 g, Sugars 3 g, Protein 22 g

Dietary Exchanges: 1 Vegetable, 3 Lean Meat

Honey–Barbecue Pork Chops

Serves 4 ▪ *1 pork chop per serving*

¼ cup mesquite- or hickory-smoked barbecue sauce (lowest sodium available)

3 tablespoons honey

½ teaspoon ground cumin

¼ teaspoon salt

⅛ teaspoon pepper

4 very thin pork loin chops with bone (about 1 pound 4 ounces), all visible fat discarded

1 teaspoon canola or corn oil

In a small bowl, stir together the barbecue sauce, honey, and cumin.

Sprinkle the salt and pepper over both sides of the pork chops. In a large nonstick skillet, heat the oil over medium-high heat, swirling to coat the bottom. Cook the pork chops for 2 minutes. Spoon half the sauce over the pork chops. Turn the pork chops. Spoon the remaining sauce over the pork chops. Cook for 2 minutes. Reduce the heat to medium. Turn the pork chops. Cook for 1 minute on each side, moving the pork chops around in the skillet to coat with the sauce, which darkens to a rich brown as it cooks.

Per Serving: Calories 224, Total Fat 9.0 g, Saturated Fat 3.0 g, Polyunsaturated Fat 1.0 g, Monounsaturated Fat 4.0 g, Cholesterol 49 mg, Sodium 293 mg, Carbohydrates 20 g, Dietary Fiber 0 g, Sugars 19 g, Protein 15 g

Dietary Exchanges: 1½ Other Carbohydrate, 2 Medium-Fat Meat

Slow-Simmered Beef Pot

Serves 4 ▪ *1 cup per serving*

Vegetable oil spray
- 1 **teaspoon canola or corn oil**
- 1 **pound top round steak, all visible fat discarded, cut into 1-inch cubes**
- 1 **medium onion, cut lengthwise into eighths**
- 1 **cup water**
- 1½ **teaspoons instant coffee granules**
- ¼ **teaspoon pepper**
- 3 **medium carrots, cut crosswise into 2-inch pieces**
- 1 **medium green bell pepper and 1 medium red bell pepper, or**
  2 medium green bell peppers, cut into 1-inch squares
- 2 **tablespoons no-salt-added ketchup**
- 1 **tablespoon Italian salad dressing mix (about ½ 0.7-ounce packet)**

Lightly spray a Dutch oven with vegetable oil spray. Pour in the oil, swirling to coat the bottom. Heat over medium-high heat. Cook the steak for 3 to 4 minutes, or until beginning to brown, stirring frequently. Stir in the onion, water, coffee granules, and pepper. Increase the heat to high and bring to a boil. Reduce the heat and simmer, covered, for 45 minutes, or until the beef just begins to become slightly tender (no stirring needed).

Stir in the remaining ingredients. Increase the heat to high and bring to a boil. Reduce the heat and simmer, covered, for 30 minutes, or until the beef is very tender (no stirring needed).

Per Serving: Calories 216, Total Fat 5.0 g, Saturated Fat 1.5 g, Polyunsaturated Fat 0.5 g, Monounsaturated Fat 2.0 g, Cholesterol 64 mg, Sodium 472 mg, Carbohydrates 15 g, Dietary Fiber 3 g, Sugars 9 g, Protein 27 g

Dietary Exchanges: 3 Vegetable, 3 Lean Meat

Country-Fried Steak with Creamy Gravy

Serves 4 ▪ *3 ounces steak and 2 tablespoons gravy per serving*

½ cup low-fat buttermilk

⅓ cup all-purpose flour

2 teaspoons salt-free extra-spicy seasoning blend

⅛ teaspoon salt

1 1-pound top round cube steak, cut into 4 pieces

2 teaspoons canola or corn oil

Creamy Gravy

¼ cup all-purpose flour

2 teaspoons salt-free powdered chicken bouillon or very low sodium chicken granules

⅛ teaspoon salt (omit if using chicken granules)

2 cups fat-free milk

1 tablespoon Worcestershire sauce (lowest sodium available)

1 teaspoon chipotle pepper sauce or red hot-pepper sauce

Pour the buttermilk into a shallow bowl. In a separate shallow bowl, stir together the flour, seasoning blend, and ⅛ teaspoon salt. Set the bowls and a large plate in a row, assembly-line fashion. Dip a steak in the buttermilk, turning to coat. Put the steak in the flour mixture, turning to coat. Gently shake off the excess flour. Put the steak on the plate. Repeat with the remaining steaks.

In a large nonstick skillet, heat the oil over medium-high heat, swirling to coat the bottom. Cook the steaks for 5 to 6 minutes on each side, or until browned, being careful when turning so the coating does not stick to the skillet. Transfer to a large plate.

Meanwhile, in a small bowl, stir together the flour, bouillon, and ⅛ teaspoon salt if using. Gradually pour in the milk, whisking until smooth. Whisk in the Worcestershire sauce and pepper sauce. When the steaks are removed from the skillet, pour this mixture in. Increase the heat to high and bring to a boil, stirring often. Reduce the heat and simmer for 3 to 5 minutes, or until thickened. Add the steaks, spooning the gravy over them. Simmer, covered, for 5 minutes. Transfer the steaks and gravy to plates.

Per Serving: Calories 290, Total Fat 6.5 g, Saturated Fat 1.5 g, Polyunsaturated Fat 1.0 g, Monounsaturated Fat 3.0 g, Cholesterol 67 mg, Sodium 271 mg, Carbohydrates 23 g, Dietary Fiber 1 g, Sugars 8 g, Protein 33 g

Dietary Exchanges: 1 Starch, ½ Skim Milk, 3 Lean Meat

Meat Loaf and Brown Gravy

Serves 4 ▪ 3 ounces meat loaf and ¼ cup gravy per serving

Vegetable oil spray
1 **pound extra-lean ground beef**
¾ **medium green bell pepper, finely chopped**
½ **cup uncooked rolled oats**
Whites of 2 large eggs
¼ **teaspoon dried oregano, crumbled**
1 **0.87-ounce packet brown gravy mix (2 tablespoons reserved)**
½ **teaspoon canola or corn oil**
1 **medium onion, thinly sliced, slices cut in half**
¾ **cup cold water**
½ **teaspoon Worcestershire sauce (lowest sodium available)**
   or balsamic vinegar
¼ **teaspoon instant coffee granules**
¼ **teaspoon pepper**
⅛ **teaspoon salt**

Preheat the oven to 350°F. Lightly spray a rimmed baking sheet with vegetable oil spray.

In a medium bowl, stir together the beef, bell pepper, oats, egg whites, oregano, and all but 2 tablespoons of the gravy mix. (The remaining mix will be used later.) Place on the baking sheet and shape into an oval loaf, about 8×4 inches, smoothing the top.

Bake for 45 to 55 minutes, or until the internal temperature registers 165°F on a meat or instant-read thermometer. Remove from the oven.

Meanwhile, heat the oil in a medium nonstick skillet over medium-high heat, swirling to coat the bottom. Cook the onion for 5 to 7 minutes, or until beginning to richly brown on the edges, stirring occasionally.

In a small bowl, stir together the remaining ingredients, including the reserved 2 tablespoons gravy mix. Stir into the onions. Cook for 1 minute, or until slightly thickened, stirring constantly.

To serve, cut the meat loaf into 8 slices. Place on plates. Spoon the gravy over the meat loaf.

Per Serving: Calories 244, Total Fat 7.5 g, Saturated Fat 2.5 g, Polyunsaturated Fat 1.0 g, Monounsaturated Fat 3.0 g, Cholesterol 63 mg, Sodium 489 mg, Carbohydrates 15 g, Dietary Fiber 2 g, Sugars 3 g, Protein 29 g

Dietary Exchanges: 1 Starch, 3 Lean Meat

Vegetarian Two-Bean Chili

Serves 4 ▪ 1½ cups per serving

Vegetable oil spray
1 **teaspoon olive oil**
1 **large onion, chopped**
2 **medium garlic cloves, minced**
1 **14.5-ounce can no-salt-added stewed tomatoes with onions, celery, and bell peppers, undrained**
½ **6-ounce can no-salt-added tomato paste**
1 **15-ounce can no-salt-added black beans, undrained**
1 **15-ounce can no-salt-added dark red kidney beans, undrained**
2 **tablespoons Worcestershire sauce (lowest sodium available)**
1 **tablespoon chili powder**
1 **tablespoon salt-free extra-spicy seasoning blend**
2 **teaspoons sugar**

Lightly spray a Dutch oven with vegetable oil spray. Add the oil and swirl to coat the bottom. Add the onion and cook over medium-high heat until golden, about 3 minutes, stirring frequently. Add the garlic and cook for 10 seconds. Add the undrained tomatoes, breaking up any large pieces with a spoon. Stir in the tomato paste. Stir in the remaining ingredients. Bring to a boil, still over medium-high heat, then reduce the heat and simmer for 15 minutes, stirring occasionally.

Per Serving: Calories 266; Total Fat 1.5 g; Saturated Fat 0 g; Polyunsaturated Fat 0.5 g; Monounsaturated Fat 1 g; Cholesterol 0 mg; Sodium 48 mg; Carbohydrates 51 g; Dietary Fiber 12 g; Sugars 16 g; Protein 15 g

Dietary Exchanges: 3 Starch, 1 Vegetable, ½ Very Lean Meat

Vegetarian Entrées

Hearty Red Beans and Rice

Serves 4 ▪ *1½ cups per serving*

<table>
<tr><td>1</td><td>cup uncooked instant brown rice or ¾ cup uncooked brown or white basmati rice</td></tr>
<tr><td>2</td><td>teaspoons olive oil</td></tr>
<tr><td>1</td><td>medium onion, thinly sliced</td></tr>
<tr><td>1</td><td>medium red bell pepper, thinly sliced</td></tr>
<tr><td>2</td><td>medium ribs of celery, diced</td></tr>
<tr><td>1</td><td>medium eggplant (about 8 ounces), diced</td></tr>
<tr><td>2</td><td>medium garlic cloves, minced</td></tr>
<tr><td>1</td><td>15-ounce can no-salt-added red beans, undrained</td></tr>
<tr><td>1½</td><td>cups low-sodium vegetable broth</td></tr>
<tr><td>2</td><td>tablespoons imitation bacon bits</td></tr>
<tr><td>½</td><td>teaspoon salt</td></tr>
<tr><td>¼</td><td>teaspoon crushed red pepper flakes</td></tr>
</table>

Prepare the rice using the package directions, omitting the salt and margarine.

Heat the oil in a large nonstick skillet over medium heat, swirling to coat the bottom. Cook the onion, bell pepper, and celery for 2 to 3 minutes, or until tender-crisp, stirring occasionally. Stir in the eggplant and garlic. Cook for 4 to 5 minutes, or until the eggplant is tender. Add water, 1 tablespoon at a time, if the eggplant sticks to the pan. Stir in the remaining ingredients. Increase the heat to medium high and bring to a simmer. Reduce the heat and simmer, covered, for 10 to 15 minutes, or until the flavors blend, stirring occasionally.

Per Serving: Calories 244, Total Fat 4.0 g, Saturated Fat 0.5 g, Polyunsaturated Fat 0.5 g, Monounsaturated Fat 2.0 g, Cholesterol 0 mg, Sodium 393 mg, Carbohydrates 42 g, Dietary Fiber 9 g, Sugars 6 g, Protein 10 g

Dietary Exchanges: 2 Starch, 3 Vegetable, ½ Fat

Curried Vegetable Casserole

Serves 4 ▪ *1½ cups per serving*

Vegetable oil spray
2 **teaspoons olive oil**
½ **medium red bell pepper, thinly sliced**
½ **medium onion, thinly sliced**
1 **small yellow summer squash, thinly sliced**
1 **small zucchini, thinly sliced**
½ **cup frozen corn, thawed**
½ **cup frozen peas, thawed**
1 **10¾-ounce can reduced-fat, reduced-sodium cream of celery soup**
1 **cup fat-free half-and-half**
1 **cup low-sodium vegetable broth**
1 **teaspoon curry powder**
¼ **teaspoon salt**
¼ **teaspoon pepper**
1 **cup uncooked instant brown rice**

Preheat the oven to 375°F. Lightly spray a 13×9×2-inch metal baking pan with vegetable oil spray. (If using glass, reduce the heat to 350°F.)

Heat the oil in a large skillet over medium heat, swirling to coat the bottom. Cook the bell pepper and onion for 2 to 3 minutes, or until tender-crisp, stirring occasionally. Stir in the yellow summer squash and zucchini. Cook for 4 to 5 minutes, or until the vegetables are tender, stirring occasionally. Stir in the corn and peas. Remove from the heat.

Meanwhile, in a large bowl, whisk together the remaining ingredients except the rice.

Stir the vegetable mixture and rice into the soup mixture, combining thoroughly. Spoon into the baking pan. Bake, covered, for 40 to 45 minutes, or until the rice is tender.

Per Serving: Calories 249, Total Fat 4.5 g, Saturated Fat 1.0 g, Polyunsaturated Fat 0.5 g, Monounsaturated Fat 2.0 g, Cholesterol 3 mg, Sodium 517 mg, Carbohydrates 45 g, Dietary Fiber 4 g, Sugars 11 g, Protein 10 g

Dietary Exchanges: 3½ Starch, 1 Vegetable, ½ Fat

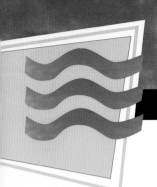

Green Beans and Red Potatoes

Serves 6 ▪ ½ cup per serving

8   ounces green beans,
       trimmed and cut into 2-inch pieces
8   ounces red potatoes, cut into ½-inch cubes
2   tablespoons snipped fresh parsley
1   tablespoon plus
       1½ teaspoons light tub margarine
¼   teaspoon salt
⅛   teaspoon pepper, or to taste
⅛   teaspoon paprika

In a large saucepan, steam the green beans and potatoes for
8 minutes, or until the potatoes are tender. Transfer to a medium
serving bowl. Add the remaining ingredients. Stir until the paprika
is distributed.

Per Serving: Calories 50, Total Fat 1.0 g, Saturated Fat 0.0 g, Polyunsaturated Fat 0.5 g,
Monounsaturated Fat 0.5 g, Cholesterol 0 mg, Sodium 125 mg, Carbohydrates 9 g,
Dietary Fiber 2 g, Sugars 1 g, Protein 2 g

Dietary Exchanges: ½ Starch

Vegetables
& Sides

Oven-Fried Green Tomatoes

Serves 4 ▪ *2 tomato slices per serving*

Vegetable oil spray
2 **large green tomatoes, about 2 inches high (about 1 pound)**
1 **tablespoon olive oil**
½ **cup yellow cornmeal (stone-ground preferred)**
Paprika, to taste
¼ **teaspoon salt**

Preheat the oven to 425°F. Line a baking sheet with aluminum foil and lightly spray with vegetable oil spray.

Cut and discard a thin slice from the top and bottom of each tomato. Cut each tomato into 4 slices, each about ½ inch thick.

Pour the oil into a shallow bowl or plate. Put the cornmeal in another shallow bowl or plate. Set the two bowls and the baking sheet in a row, assembly-line fashion.

Lightly coat a tomato slice with the oil, then with the cornmeal, shaking off any excess. Place the tomato slice on the baking sheet. Repeat with the remaining tomato slices. Sprinkle lightly with paprika and half the salt. Using the prongs of a fork, gently turn the slices and repeat.

Bake for 10 minutes. Turn the slices. Bake for 8 minutes, or until tender. Remove from the oven. Turn the slices. Let stand for 3 to 4 minutes so the tomatoes will soften slightly.

Per Serving: Calories 112; Total Fat 4 g; Saturated Fat 0.5 g; Polyunsaturated Fat 0.5 g; Monounsaturated Fat 2.5 g; Cholesterol 0 mg; Sodium 158 mg; Carbohydrates 19 g; Dietary Fiber 2 g; Sugars 4 g; Protein 3 g

Dietary Exchanges: 1 Starch, 1 Vegetable, ½ Fat

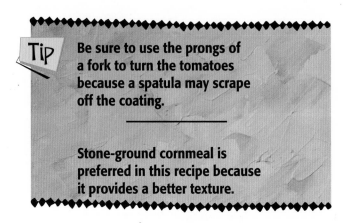

Tip

Be sure to use the prongs of a fork to turn the tomatoes because a spatula may scrape off the coating.

Stone-ground cornmeal is preferred in this recipe because it provides a better texture.

Candied Sweet Potatoes

Serves 6 ▪ *½ cup per serving*

Vegetable oil spray
2   **medium sweet potatoes (about 2 pounds total), quartered**
1   **8-ounce can crushed pineapple in its own juice, undrained**
½   **cup fresh orange juice**
¼   **cup firmly packed light brown sugar**
1   **tablespoon cornstarch**
1   **tablespoon light tub margarine**

Topping

2   **tablespoons firmly packed light brown sugar**
1   **tablespoon light tub margarine, melted**
¼   **cup all-purpose flour**
¼   **cup chopped pecans**
¼   **teaspoon ground cinnamon**

Lightly spray a 1½-quart shallow baking dish with vegetable oil spray.

Put the sweet potatoes in a large saucepan. Add water to cover. Bring to a boil over high heat and boil for 25 to 30 minutes, or until tender. Remove from the pan and let cool for 5 minutes. Discard the skins. Cut the potatoes into ¼-inch-thick slices. Place in the baking dish.

Meanwhile, in a small saucepan, stir together the pineapple, orange juice, ¼ cup brown sugar, cornstarch, and 1 tablespoon margarine. Cook over medium heat for 6 to 8 minutes, or until the mixture comes to a boil and thickens, stirring frequently. Reduce the heat and simmer for 5 minutes, stirring occasionally.

Preheat the oven to 350°F.

In a small bowl, combine the topping ingredients. Spoon the pineapple mixture over the sweet potatoes. Sprinkle with the topping. Bake for 30 to 35 minutes, or until heated through.

Per Serving: Calories 318; Total Fat 5 g; Saturated Fat 0.5 g; Polyunsaturated Fat 1.5 g; Monounsaturated Fat 3 g; Cholesterol 0 mg; Sodium 91 mg; Carbohydrates 64 g; Dietary Fiber 6 g; Sugars 28 g; Protein 4 g

Dietary Exchanges: 4 Starch, ½ Fruit

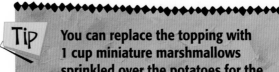

Tip You can replace the topping with 1 cup miniature marshmallows sprinkled over the potatoes for the last 5 minutes of baking or omit both the topping and the marshmallows.

Collard Greens with Smoked Sausage

Serves 8 ▪ *½ cup per serving*

1	teaspoon olive oil
4	ounces low-fat smoked turkey sausage, cut into ¼-inch cubes
1	teaspoon olive oil
1	medium onion, finely chopped
1	14.5-ounce can fat-free, low-sodium chicken broth
1	pound frozen chopped collard greens
1½	teaspoons sugar
¼	teaspoon salt

Heat a large saucepan over medium heat. Add 1 teaspoon oil and swirl to coat the bottom. Cook the sausage for 2 to 3 minutes, or until the edges begin to richly brown, stirring frequently. Transfer to a plate; do not drain the pan.

Add 1 teaspoon oil to the pan. Cook the onion for 3 minutes, or until soft, stirring frequently. Stir in the broth. Increase the heat to high and bring to a boil. Stir in the collard greens. Return to a boil. Reduce the heat and simmer, covered, for 25 minutes, or until the greens are tender. Remove from the heat.

Stir in the sausage, sugar, and salt. Let stand, covered, for 10 minutes.

Per Serving: Calories 55; Total Fat 1.5 g; Saturated Fat 0.5 g; Polyunsaturated Fat 0 g; Monounsaturated Fat 1.5 g; Cholesterol 5 mg; Sodium 263 mg; Carbohydrates 7 g; Dietary Fiber 2 g; Sugars 3 g; Protein 4 g

Dietary Exchanges: 1½ Vegetable, ½ Lean Meat

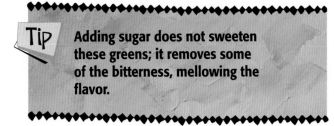

Tip Adding sugar does not sweeten these greens; it removes some of the bitterness, mellowing the flavor.

Okra and Tomatoes

Serves 6 ▪ *½ cup per serving*

2	teaspoons olive oil
½	medium onion, chopped
½	medium green bell pepper, chopped
½	medium rib of celery, chopped
1	14.5-ounce can no-salt-added tomatoes, undrained
10	ounces fresh okra, cut into ½-inch slices, or frozen sliced okra, thawed
½	teaspoon sugar
¼	teaspoon dried thyme, crumbled
½	teaspoon salt, divided use

Heat a large saucepan over medium-high heat. Add the oil and swirl to coat the bottom. Cook the onion, bell pepper, and celery for 4 minutes, or until the onion is soft, stirring frequently. Stir in the remaining ingredients except ¼ teaspoon salt. Bring to a boil. Reduce the heat and simmer, covered, for 15 minutes, or until the okra is very tender, stirring occasionally. Remove from the heat.

Stir in ¼ teaspoon salt. Let stand, covered, for 5 minutes.

Per Serving: Calories 50; Total Fat 1.5 g; Saturated Fat 0 g; Polyunsaturated Fat 0 g; Monounsaturated Fat 1 g; Cholesterol 0 mg; Sodium 208 mg; Carbohydrates 8 g; Dietary Fiber 3 g; Sugars 4 g; Protein 2 g

Dietary Exchanges: 1½ Vegetable, ½ Fat

Rich and Creamy Mac and Cheese

Serves 4 ▪ *½ cup per serving*

- **4 ounces dried elbow macaroni**
- **4 slices low-fat American cheese, about ¾ ounce each**
- **⅓ cup fat-free milk**
- **2 tablespoons light tub margarine**
- **1 teaspoon prepared mustard**
- **½ teaspoon Worcestershire sauce (lowest sodium available)**
- **⅛ teaspoon salt**
- **⅛ teaspoon red hot-pepper sauce**

In a large saucepan, prepare the macaroni using the package directions, omitting the salt and oil. Drain well in a colander. Return to the pan.

Add the remaining ingredients, stirring until the cheese melts. Cook over medium heat for 8 to 10 minutes, or until slightly thickened, stirring frequently. Remove from the heat. Let stand for 5 minutes to continue to thicken.

Per Serving: Calories 173; Total Fat 3.5 g; Saturated Fat 0.5 g; Polyunsaturated Fat 0.5 g; Monounsaturated Fat 1.5 g; Cholesterol 5 mg; Sodium 344 mg; Carbohydrates 24 g; Dietary Fiber 1 g; Sugars 3 g; Protein 9 g

Dietary Exchanges: 1½ Starch, 1 Lean Meat

Fiery Smothered Cabbage

Serves 4 ▪ *½ cup per serving*

- **1   small Napa cabbage**
- **1   tablespoon olive oil**
- **1   cup coarsely chopped onion**
- **1   ounce extra-lean ham (lowest sodium available) or
    2 ounces smoked turkey breast (lowest sodium available),
    cut into bite-size cubes**
- **1   cup fat-free, low-sodium chicken broth**
- **1   ounce dry white wine (regular or nonalcoholic)**
- **½   to 1 teaspoon black pepper**
- **1½   teaspoons salt-free herb seasoning blend, such as garlic-herb**
- **1   teaspoon crushed red pepper flakes**
- **¼   teaspoon onion powder**
- **¼   teaspoon garlic powder**
- **¼   teaspoon salt**
- **1   small red bell pepper, cut lengthwise into thin strips**

Discard the outer leaves of the cabbage. Cut the remaining cabbage into quarters. Cut out and discard the core from each portion. Cut enough of the remaining leaves in long, fine shreds to measure 2 cups; do not chop.

Pour the oil into a large skillet and swirl to coat the bottom. Heat over medium heat. Cook the onion for about 2 minutes, or until it begins to soften, stirring frequently. Stir in the ham. Cook for about 1 minute, continuing to stir. Add the cabbage. Stir to combine. Stir in the broth, white wine, and black pepper. Bring to a simmer and cook for 5 minutes, or until the cabbage just begins to soften. Stir in the remaining ingredients except the bell pepper strips. Place the strips on the cabbage mixture. Reduce the heat and simmer, covered, for about 5 minutes, or until the strips have slightly softened.

Prepared with Ham—Per Serving: Calories 77; Total Fat 3.5 g; Saturated Fat 0.5 g; Polyunsaturated Fat 0.5 g; Monounsaturated Fat 2.5 g; Cholesterol 3 mg; Sodium 227 mg; Carbohydrates 7 g; Dietary Fiber 2 g; Sugars 3 g; Protein 3 g

Dietary Exchanges: 1½ Vegetable, 1 Fat

Prepared with Turkey—Per Serving: Calories 84; Total Fat 4 g; Saturated Fat 0.5 g; Polyunsaturated Fat 0.5 g; Monounsaturated Fat 2.5 g; Cholesterol 8 mg; Sodium 290 mg; Carbohydrates 8 g; Dietary Fiber 2 g; Sugars 4 g; Protein 4 g

Dietary Exchanges: 1½ Vegetable, 1 Fat

Slow-Cooker Pinto Beans

Serves 12 ▪ *½ cup per serving*

- **8 ounces dried pinto beans (about 1¼ cups)**
- **3 cups fat-free, low-sodium chicken broth**
- **1 small carrot, chopped**
- **½ medium rib of celery, chopped**
- **¼ medium onion, chopped**
- **2 ounces reduced-fat smoked sausage (lowest fat and sodium available), diced**
- **2 tablespoons imitation bacon bits**
- **1 medium jalapeño pepper, ribs and seeds discarded, diced (use plastic gloves while handling)**
- **½ teaspoon salt**
- **¼ teaspoon pepper**

Sort through the beans, removing any shriveled beans or stones. Put the beans in a large bowl and cover with cold water by 2 inches. Let soak for 3 to 12 hours. Drain in a colander. Transfer to a slow cooker.

Stir in the remaining ingredients. Cook, covered, on high for 4 to 5 hours or on low for 8 to 10 hours, or until the beans and vegetables are tender. If the mixture gets too dry, add water ½ cup at a time. (If your cooker does not have a glass lid, check after about 2 hours if cooking on high, or about 4 hours if cooking on low. Continue checking about every 30 minutes.) Ladle the beans and pot likker (cooking liquid) into bowls.

Per Serving: Calories 81, Total Fat 1.0 g, Saturated Fat 0.0 g, Polyunsaturated Fat 0.0 g, Monounsaturated Fat 0.5 g, Cholesterol 3 mg, Sodium 175 mg, Carbohydrates 13 g, Dietary Fiber 4 g, Sugars 1 g, Protein 6 g

Dietary Exchanges: 1 Starch, ½ Very Lean Meat

Tip Substitute three 15-ounce cans no-salt-added pinto beans with their liquid for the dried beans. Pour into a large saucepan. Add the remaining ingredients, reducing the broth to 1½ cups. Bring to a simmer over medium-high heat, stirring occasionally. Reduce the heat and simmer, covered, for 15 to 20 minutes, or until the vegetables are tender and the flavors blend.

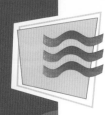

Broccoli Cheese Casserole

Serves 8 ▪ *½ cup per serving*

Vegetable oil spray
1 **pound fresh broccoli florets**
½ **cup water**
1 **2-ounce jar pimientos, drained**
½ **cup fat-free milk**
½ **cup fat-free, low-sodium chicken broth**
1 **tablespoon plus 1½ teaspoons all-purpose flour**
½ **teaspoon onion powder**
¼ **teaspoon salt**
¼ **teaspoon pepper**
⅛ **teaspoon cayenne**
½ **cup shredded reduced-fat Cheddar cheese**
2 **tablespoons shredded or grated Parmesan cheese**
2 **tablespoons chopped walnuts**
¼ **cup plain dry bread crumbs**

Preheat the oven to 350°F. Lightly spray a shallow 1½-quart casserole dish with vegetable oil spray.

In a medium saucepan, bring the broccoli and water to a boil over medium-high heat. Reduce the heat and simmer, covered, for 2 minutes, or until the broccoli is tender-crisp. Using a slotted spoon, transfer the broccoli to the casserole dish. Discard the water. Stir the pimientos into the broccoli.

In a small bowl, whisk together the milk, broth, flour, onion powder, salt, pepper, and cayenne until blended (a few lumps of flour may remain). Pour into the same saucepan. Bring to a simmer over medium-high heat, whisking constantly. Cook for 1 to 2 minutes, or until thickened, whisking constantly. Remove from the heat.

Add the Cheddar and Parmesan, whisking for 30 seconds, or until melted. Pour over the broccoli. Sprinkle with the walnuts, then the bread crumbs.

Bake for 20 to 25 minutes, or until the mixture is warmed through and the topping is golden brown.

Per Serving: Calories 80, Total Fat 3.0 g, Saturated Fat 1.5 g, Polyunsaturated Fat 1.0 g, Monounsaturated Fat 0.5 g, Cholesterol 5 mg, Sodium 190 mg, Carbohydrates 8 g, Dietary Fiber 2 g, Sugars 1 g, Protein 6 g

Dietary Exchanges: 1½ Vegetable, ½ Very Lean Meat, ½ Fat

Sweet Potato Muffins

Serves 24 ▪ *1 muffin per serving*

Vegetable oil spray (optional)
1 **18.5-ounce package spice cake mix**
1 **13-ounce can sweet potatoes packed with no liquid or in light syrup, drained if needed**
½ **cup uncooked quick-cooking oatmeal**
½ **cup egg substitute**
½ **cup water**
2 **teaspoons grated orange zest**
½ **cup fresh orange juice**
1 **tablespoon ground cinnamon**

Preheat the oven to 350°F. Lightly spray two 12-cup muffin pans with vegetable oil spray or put paper muffin cups in the pans.

In a large mixing bowl, stir all the ingredients together. Using an electric mixer, beat according to the package directions. Spoon the batter into the muffin cups.

Bake for 22 to 24 minutes, or until a cake tester or wooden toothpick inserted in the center of a muffin in the middle of the pan comes out clean. Transfer the muffins from the pans to a cooling rack. Let cool for 15 to 20 minutes before serving.

Per Serving: Calories 115, Total Fat 1.5 g, Saturated Fat 1.0 g, Polyunsaturated Fat 0.0 g, Monounsaturated Fat 0.5 g, Cholesterol 0 mg, Sodium 159 mg, Carbohydrates 24 g, Dietary Fiber 1 g, Sugars 12 g, Protein 2 g

Dietary Exchanges: 1½ Other Carbohydrate, ½ Fat

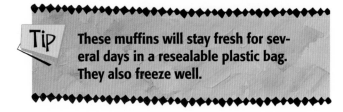

Tip These muffins will stay fresh for several days in a resealable plastic bag. They also freeze well.

Breads
& Breakfasts

Skillet Ham Hash

Serves 4 ▪ *1 cup per serving*

2   **teaspoons olive oil**

1   **large green bell pepper, diced**

1   **large red bell pepper, diced**

1   **medium onion, diced**

½   **cup diced lower-sodium, low-fat ham (about 4 ounces), all visible fat discarded**

3   **cups frozen fat-free southern-style diced hash brown potatoes, thawed**

½   **teaspoon salt-free Cajun or Creole seasoning blend**

2   **tablespoons snipped fresh parsley**

¼   **teaspoon salt**

¼   **teaspoon pepper**

In a large nonstick skillet, heat the oil over medium heat, swirling to coat the bottom. Cook the bell peppers and onion for 4 to 5 minutes, or until tender, stirring occasionally. Stir in the ham. Cook for 1 to 2 minutes, or until warmed through, stirring occasionally.

Stir in the hash browns and seasoning blend. Cook without stirring for 4 minutes, or until the bottom is golden brown. Stir (the golden-brown pieces will be redistributed). Cook without stirring for 4 minutes, or until the bottom is golden brown and the mixture is warmed through.

Stir in the parsley, salt, and pepper. Spoon onto plates.

Per Serving: Calories 207, Total Fat 3.5 g, Saturated Fat 0.5 g, Polyunsaturated Fat 0.5 g, Monounsaturated Fat 2.0 g, Cholesterol 12 mg, Sodium 420 mg, Carbohydrates 37 g, Dietary Fiber 5 g, Sugars 6 g, Protein 9 g

Dietary Exchanges: 2 Starch, 1½ Vegetable, ½ Lean Meat

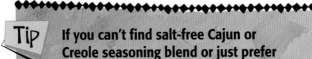

Tip   **If you can't find salt-free Cajun or Creole seasoning blend or just prefer to make your own, stir together 1 teaspoon each chile powder, onion powder, garlic powder, dried thyme, paprika, and ground cumin in a small bowl. Makes 2 tablespoons. Store in an airtight container for up to 6 months.**

Southern Cornbread

Serves 9 ▪ *1 piece per serving*

Vegetable oil spray
1 **cup yellow cornmeal**
½ **cup all-purpose flour**
½ **cup whole-wheat flour**
2 **tablespoons sugar**
½ **teaspoon baking soda**
½ **teaspoon baking powder**
½ **teaspoon salt**
1 **cup no-salt-added cream-style corn, undrained**
½ **cup frozen whole-kernel corn, thawed**
½ **cup fat-free or low-fat buttermilk**
¼ **cup fat-free milk**
   Egg substitute equivalent to 1 egg
2 **tablespoons canola or corn oil**

Preheat the oven to 425°F. Lightly spray a 9-inch square or round baking pan or pie pan with vegetable oil spray.

In a large bowl, stir together the cornmeal, both flours, sugar, baking soda, baking powder, and salt. Make a well in the center.

In a medium bowl, stir together the remaining ingredients. Pour into the well in the flour mixture, stirring just until moistened. Spoon into the baking pan. Lightly spray the top of the batter with vegetable oil spray.

Bake for 20 to 25 minutes, or until a wooden toothpick or cake tester comes out clean when inserted in the center. Transfer the pan to a cooling rack and let cool for 5 to 10 minutes before slicing.

Per Serving: Calories 181; Total Fat 4 g; Saturated Fat 0.5 g; Polyunsaturated Fat 1 g; Monounsaturated Fat 2 g; Cholesterol 1 mg; Sodium 255 mg; Carbohydrates 34 g; Dietary Fiber 3 g; Sugars 5 g; Protein 5 g

Dietary Exchanges: 2½ Starch, ½ Fat

Angel Biscuits

Serves 26 ▪ *1 biscuit per serving*

¼	**cup lukewarm water (105°F to 115°F)**
1	**¼-ounce package active dry yeast**
½	**teaspoon sugar**
2½	**cups all-purpose flour**
2	**tablespoons sugar**
½	**teaspoon baking powder**
½	**teaspoon baking soda**
⅓	**cup canola or corn oil**
1	**cup fat-free or low-fat buttermilk**
¼	**cup all-purpose flour, plus more as needed**
	Vegetable oil spray

In a medium bowl, stir together the water, yeast, and ½ teaspoon sugar until the yeast is dissolved. Let the mixture stand at room temperature for 5 minutes to activate the yeast (it should smell slightly fermented).

Meanwhile, in a large bowl, whisk together 2½ cups flour, 2 tablespoons sugar, baking powder, and baking soda. Using a pastry blender or fork, cut in the oil until the mixture is crumbly, with pieces about pea size.

In a small saucepan, heat the buttermilk over medium-low heat for 1 to 2 minutes, or until it reaches 110°F on an instant-read thermometer. Or microwave the buttermilk in a microwaveable container on 100 percent power (high) for 10 to 15 seconds, or until it reaches 110°F.

Stir the buttermilk into the yeast mixture. Then stir into the flour mixture until just moistened. The dough will be slightly sticky. (Do not overmix or the biscuits will be tough.) Cover and chill for 1 hour.

Sprinkle a flat work surface with about 2 tablespoons of the remaining flour. Put the dough on the floured surface. Sprinkle the dough with 2 tablespoons flour and knead three or four times. (If the dough is too sticky, add flour, 1 tablespoon at a time.) Shape into a flat disk. With floured hands or a floured rolling pin, pat or roll the dough to ½-inch thickness. Using a floured 2½-inch round cookie cutter or glass, cut out 26 biscuits.

Lightly spray a rimmed baking sheet with vegetable oil spray. Place the biscuits in a single layer on the baking sheet (the sides of the biscuits can touch). Cover the biscuits with a dry dish towel. Let rise in a warm, draft-free place for 1 hour, or until almost doubled in size.

Preheat the oven to 450°F. Bake for 10 to 12 minutes, or until the biscuits are golden brown and a wooden toothpick or cake tester inserted into the center comes out clean.

Per Serving: Calories 83; Total Fat 3 g; Saturated Fat 0.5 g; Polyunsaturated Fat 1 g; Monounsaturated Fat 2 g; Cholesterol 0 mg; Sodium 42 mg; Carbohydrates 12 g; Dietary Fiber 0 g; Sugars 2 g; Protein 2 g

Dietary Exchanges: 1 Starch, ½ Fat

Tip

To make the dough in advance, prepare as directed on page 72 through stirring the buttermilk-yeast mixture into the flour mixture. At this point, cover the bowl with a dish towel. Let rise at room temperature for 30 minutes to activate the yeast. Remove the towel. Cover the bowl tightly with plastic wrap and refrigerate for up to 3 days. When ready to make the biscuits, shape the dough and cut as directed on page 72. Let rise for 1 to 1½ hours, or until almost doubled in size. Bake as directed above.

Creamy Cheese Grits

Serves 4 ▪ ½ cup per serving

2¼ **cups water**
 ½ **cup quick-cooking grits**
 2 **slices low-fat American cheese, about ¾ ounce each**
 2 **tablespoons fat-free milk**
 1 **tablespoon light tub margarine**
 ¼ **teaspoon salt**
 ½ **teaspoon Worcestershire sauce (lowest sodium available)**
 ⅛ **teaspoon garlic powder (optional)**
    Pepper to taste (optional)

In a medium saucepan, bring the water to a rolling boil over high heat. Stir in the grits. Reduce the heat and simmer, covered, for 9 minutes, or until very thick, stirring occasionally. (This is a longer cooking time than directed on most packages because a thicker consistency is desired.) Remove from the heat.

Add the remaining ingredients except the pepper, stirring until the cheese has completely melted. Sprinkle with the pepper.

Per Serving: Calories 105; Total Fat 2 g; Saturated Fat 0.5 g; Polyunsaturated Fat 0.5 g; Monounsaturated Fat 0.5 g; Cholesterol 3 mg; Sodium 275 mg; Carbohydrates 17 g; Dietary Fiber 0 g; Sugars 1 g; Protein 5 g

Dietary Exchanges: 1 Starch, ½ Very Lean Meat

Baked Hush Puppies

Serves 24 ▪ *1 hush puppy per serving*

> **Vegetable oil spray**
> ½ **cup yellow cornmeal**
> ½ **cup all-purpose flour**
> ½ **cup frozen whole-kernel corn, thawed**
> ¼ **medium red bell pepper, finely chopped**
> 1 **teaspoon baking powder**
> ½ **teaspoon sugar**
> ¼ **teaspoon baking soda**
> ¼ **teaspoon salt**
> ¼ **teaspoon chili powder**
> ⅓ **cup fat-free or low-fat buttermilk**
> **Egg substitute equivalent to 1 egg, or 1 large egg**
> 1 **tablespoon canola or corn oil**

Preheat the oven to 425°F. Lightly spray two 12-cup mini muffin pans with vegetable oil spray.

In a medium bowl, stir together the cornmeal, flour, corn, bell pepper, baking powder, sugar, baking soda, salt, and chili powder. Make a well in the center.

Pour the buttermilk, egg substitute, and oil into the well. Stir until just moistened. (Do not overmix or the hush puppies will be tough.) Spoon the mixture into the muffin pans, filling each cup about two-thirds full.

Bake for 10 to 12 minutes, or until a wooden toothpick or cake tester inserted in the center comes out clean. Remove the hush puppies from the pan and transfer to a cooling rack. Let cool for at least 5 minutes before serving.

Per Serving: Calories 32; Total Fat 0.5 g; Saturated Fat 0 g; Polyunsaturated Fat 0 g; Monounsaturated Fat 0.5 g; Cholesterol 0 mg; Sodium 63 mg; Carbohydrates 6 g; Dietary Fiber 0 g; Sugars 1 g; Protein 1 g

Dietary Exchanges: ½ Starch

Tip A spring-loaded ice cream scoop makes easy work of filling muffin pans with batter. Available at most gourmet shops, the scoops come in a variety of sizes. Smaller ones can be used for mini muffins and cookie dough, and the larger sizes can be used for regular-size muffins.

Sweet Potato Cake with Zesty Orange Glaze

Serves 12 ▪ *3-inch square per serving*

Vegetable oil spray

Cake

1   **18.5-ounce package spice cake mix**
1   **15-ounce can sweet potatoes in light syrup, drained**
1¼ **cups water**
    Egg substitute equivalent to 1 egg, or 1 large egg
    Whites of 2 large eggs

Glaze

2   **teaspoons grated orange zest**
1   **cup fresh orange juice**
3   **tablespoons firmly packed dark brown sugar**
1½ **teaspoons cornstarch**

Preheat the oven to 350°F. Lightly spray a 13×9×2-inch baking pan with vegetable oil spray.

In a large mixing bowl, combine the cake ingredients. Using an electric mixer, beat according to the package directions. Pour the batter into the baking pan, smoothing the surface.

Bake for 30 minutes, or until a cake tester or wooden toothpick inserted in the center comes out almost clean. Transfer the pan to a cooling rack. Let the cake cool completely, about 1 hour.

Meanwhile, in a small saucepan, stir together the glaze ingredients until the cornstarch is dissolved. Bring to a boil over medium-high heat. Boil for 1 to 1½ minutes, or until thickened, stirring frequently. Remove from the heat. Let cool completely, about 20 minutes. Spoon over the cooled cake.

Per Serving: Calories 223; Total Fat 3 g; Saturated Fat 1.5 g; Polyunsaturated Fat 0 g; Monounsaturated Fat 1 g; Cholesterol 0 mg; Sodium 312 mg; Carbohydrates 47 g; Dietary Fiber 0 g; Sugars 30 g; Protein 2 g

Dietary Exchanges: 3 Other Carbohydrate, ½ Fat

Desserts

Cozy Peach Cobbler

Serves 9 ▪ *1 piece per serving*

Vegetable oil spray

Filling

¾ **cup peach nectar**
½ **cup fresh orange juice**
2 **tablespoons cornstarch**
1½ **teaspoons vanilla extract**
¼ **teaspoon ground cinnamon**
1 **29-ounce can sliced peaches, packed in juice, drained**
1 **tablespoon firmly packed light brown sugar**

Topping

1 **tablespoon light tub margarine, melted**
1 **cup buttermilk pancake mix, whole-wheat preferred**
⅔ **cup all-purpose flour**
½ **cup sugar**
½ **teaspoon grated orange zest**
⅔ **cup fat-free evaporated milk**
2 **tablespoons firmly packed light brown sugar**
¼ **teaspoon ground cinnamon**

Preheat the oven to 400°F. Lightly spray an 8-inch square glass baking dish with vegetable oil spray.

In a medium saucepan, stir together the nectar, orange juice, cornstarch, vanilla, and cinnamon. Cook over medium heat for 6 to 8 minutes, or until the mixture comes to a boil and thickens, stirring frequently. Reduce the heat to medium low. Stir in the peaches and 1 tablespoon brown sugar. Reduce the heat and simmer for 5 minutes, stirring occasionally. Pour into the baking dish.

Meanwhile, in a medium bowl, stir together the margarine, pancake mix, flour, and sugar. Add the orange zest to the evaporated milk. Stir into the pancake mixture. Drop the dough by spoonfuls to form mounds on the warm fruit mixture.

In small bowl, combine the remaining brown sugar and cinnamon. Sprinkle over the cobbler.

Bake for 15 to 20 minutes, or until golden brown. Transfer the pan to a cooling rack and let cool for 10 minutes. Cut into squares. Serve warm or at room temperature.

Per Serving: Calories 226; Total Fat 1 g; Saturated Fat 0 g;
Polyunsaturated Fat 0 g; Monounsaturated Fat 0.5 g;
Cholesterol 1 mg; Sodium 154 mg; Carbohydrates 51 g;
Dietary Fiber 2 g; Sugars 30 g; Protein 2 g

Dietary Exchanges: 1½ Starch, 1 Fruit,
1 Other Carbohydrate

Tip If you don't find canned fruit
nectars with the other fruit juices
in the supermarket, look in the
health food or Mexican food
sections.

Coconut Layer Cake

Serves 12 ▪ *1 slice per serving*

Vegetable oil spray
1 **18.5-ounce package white cake mix**
1¼ **cups water**
1 **6-ounce jar baby food pureed pears**
Whites of 3 large eggs
½ **cup fat-free or light plain yogurt**
¼ **cup unsifted confectioners' sugar**
2 **to 3 teaspoons grated lemon zest**
2 **tablespoons fresh lemon juice**
1 **or 2 drops yellow food coloring (optional)**
8 **ounces (about 3 cups) frozen fat-free or light whipped topping, thawed in refrigerator, divided**
3 **to 4 tablespoons sweetened flaked coconut**

Preheat the oven to 350°F. Lightly spray two 9-inch round cake pans with vegetable oil spray.

In a medium bowl, combine the cake mix, water, pears, and egg whites. Using an electric mixer, beat according to the package directions. Pour the batter into the cake pans, smoothing the tops.

Bake for 22 minutes, or until a cake tester or wooden toothpick inserted in the center comes out clean. Transfer the pans to cooling racks. Let cool for 10 minutes. Turn the cake onto the racks and let cool completely, about 1 hour.

Meanwhile, in a medium bowl, stir together the yogurt, confectioners' sugar, lemon zest, lemon juice, and food coloring. Fold in 1 cup of the whipped topping until completely blended. Cover and refrigerate until needed. Refrigerate the remaining whipped topping separately.

Place one cake layer on a large plate. Top with the yogurt mixture, then with the remaining cake layer. Spread the remaining whipped topping over the side and top of the cake. Sprinkle the top with the coconut. Refrigerate until ready to serve.

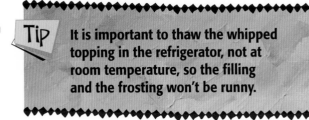

Tip It is important to thaw the whipped topping in the refrigerator, not at room temperature, so the filling and the frosting won't be runny.

Per Serving: Calories 249; Total Fat 4.5 g; Saturated Fat 2 g; Polyunsaturated Fat 0 g; Monounsaturated Fat 1 g; Cholesterol 0 mg; Sodium 331 mg; Carbohydrates 47 g; Dietary Fiber 1 g; Sugars 27 g; Protein 4 g

Dietary Exchanges: 3 Other Carbohydrate, 1 Fat

Orange Pound Cake with Mixed Berries

Serves 16 ▪ *2 (½-inch) slices cake and scant 3 tablespoons
berry mixture per serving*

Cake

  1 **16-ounce pound cake mix**
 ¾ **cup fat-free milk**
    Whites of 4 large eggs or ½ cup egg substitute
 ¼ **cup all-fruit apricot spread**
  1 **tablespoon plus 1 teaspoon grated orange zest**

Topping

 16 **ounces frozen mixed berries**
 ¼ **cup fresh orange juice**
 ½ **cup all-fruit apricot fruit spread**

Preheat the oven to 350°F.

In a medium mixing bowl, stir together the cake ingredients. Using an electric mixer, beat according to the package directions. Pour the batter into 2 nonstick 8½×4½×2½-inch loaf pans, smoothing the tops.

Bake for 27 minutes, or until a cake tester or wooden toothpick inserted in the center comes out almost clean. Transfer the pans to cooling racks. Let cool for 10 minutes. Invert the cake onto the racks and let cool completely, about 1 hour.

Meanwhile, in a medium bowl, stir together the frozen berries and orange juice.

In a small microwaveable bowl, microwave the ½ cup fruit spread on 100 percent power (high) for 20 seconds, or until melted. Gently stir into the berry mixture. Cover with plastic wrap. Let stand for 1 hour so the berries thaw and the flavors blend. Refrigerate until serving time.

To serve, cut the cake into ¹/₂-inch slices. Transfer to dessert plates. Top each serving with the berry mixture.

Per Serving: Calories 182, Total Fat 4.5 g, Saturated Fat 1.0 g, Polyunsaturated Fat 0.0 g, Monounsaturated Fat 0.0 g, Cholesterol 0 mg, Sodium 170 mg, Carbohydrates 33 g, Dietary Fiber 1 g, Sugars 20 g, Protein 3 g

Dietary Exchanges: 2 Other Carbohydrate, 1 Fat

Bananas Foster Rice Pudding

Serves 4 ▪ *½ cup per serving*

- ¾ cup fat-free half-and-half
- ½ cup uncooked quick-cooking brown rice
- ¼ cup golden raisins
- ¼ cup firmly packed dark or light brown sugar
- 1 teaspoon grated orange zest
- 2 tablespoons fresh orange juice
- 1 tablespoon light tub margarine
- ½ teaspoon ground cinnamon
- ½ teaspoon rum extract
- ⅛ teaspoon ground nutmeg
- 2 medium bananas, cut crosswise into ½-inch slices

In a medium saucepan, bring the half-and-half, rice, and raisins to a simmer over medium-high heat, stirring occasionally. Reduce the heat and simmer, covered, for 10 minutes, or until the rice is tender. Remove the pan from the heat. Cover to keep warm.

Meanwhile, in a medium skillet, stir together the remaining ingredients except the bananas. Cook over medium heat for 3 to 5 minutes, or until the mixture is warmed through and the brown sugar is dissolved, stirring occasionally. Stir in the bananas. Cook for 2 to 3 minutes, or until the bananas are warmed through, stirring occasionally.

Pour the banana mixture into the rice mixture. Stir gently to combine. Spoon into bowls. Serve warm.

Per Serving: Calories 225, Total Fat 2.0 g, Saturated Fat 0.0 g, Polyunsaturated Fat 0.5 g, Monounsaturated Fat 1.0 g, Cholesterol 0 mg, Sodium 77 mg, Carbohydrates 51 g, Dietary Fiber 3 g, Sugars 30 g, Protein 5 g

Dietary Exchanges: 1½ Fruit, 2 Other Carbohydrate, ½ Fat

American Heart Association® | American Stroke Association®

POWER TO END STROKE℠
You are the Power

Power To End Stroke is an education and awareness campaign that embraces and celebrates the culture, energy, creativity, and lifestyles of African Americans. The American Stroke Association, a division of the American Heart Association, invites you to join us in reducing the incidence of stroke in our communities.

Cardiovascular disease, including stroke, causes about 33 percent of all deaths among African American men and 40 percent among women. In a recent survey, the American Stroke Association found that although 70 percent of African American adults felt they were knowledgeable about stroke, only 30 percent knew how to define it correctly. Blacks are almost twice as likely as whites to have a first stroke, yet only about 50 percent of the respondents knew the symptoms.

You can help improve these numbers. Join the movement and feel the power:

Put down the cigarettes and stop smoking.

Observe advice from your doctor and know your family's medical history.

Watch your weight and be physically active at least 30 minutes on 5 or more days of the week.

Eat healthfully and avoid foods high in saturated fat, trans fat, cholesterol, and sodium.

Regulate and control high blood pressure, high blood cholesterol, and diabetes.

GO FOR THE GOAL

You have the power to fight stroke—and win! Take these steps to make a personal commitment to end stroke.

■ **Take the Pledge and learn the warning signs.** Make your own statement to not just survive, but thrive! See page 91 for details on taking the Pledge and information about the warning signs of stroke.

■ **Be proud and pass it on: Host a Family Reunion.** Once you've joined, you can help advance the cause by spreading the word to your family and friends. We make it easy with our downloadable Family Reunion Toolkit.

■ **Plan a Power Sunday.** Our places of worship are the heart of our community, not only providing spiritual comfort but also serving as the support center for social, educational, and health issues. Ask your church to participate in a Power Sunday by discussing stroke awareness with the congregation.

■ **Keep the beat with "Keep On Pushin' (The Power Song)."** Download this inspirational recording by the platinum-selling, Grammy-nominated R&B group AZ YET. Each iTunes download will help fund the Power To End Stroke campaign.

■ **Shop Power.** Support the Power To End Stroke movement by visiting our online store at **shoppower.org**. Every purchase contributes to the fight against stroke in African Americans.

For more information on the American Stroke Association or how you can join the movement to fight stroke, call **1-888-4-STROKE** or visit **StrokeAssociation.org/power**. Find out what's happening near you by visiting **local.StrokeAssociation.org** and make a difference!

Follow the three "Rs" to help protect yourself against stroke.

- **Reduce your risk.** Learn about the risk factors for stroke and work with your doctor to make lifestyle changes.

- **Recognize the signs of a stroke.** Stroke is a medical emergency—every second counts!

- **Respond quickly.** Call 9-1-1 immediately if you or someone nearby shows the warning signs or symptoms of stroke. Then check the time that the first symptoms started. You'll need this information later.

Knowledge Is Power

Stroke and heart disease are major health risks for everyone, especially for African Americans. But you have the power to take charge of your health by making good choices.

REDUCE YOUR RISKS

Those good choices start with good information. Learn about the factors that increase your risk for cardiovascular disease and what you can do about them. Some factors—such as increasing age and family history—can't be changed, but many can. **You have the power to affect these major risk factors: smoking, high blood pressure, high blood cholesterol, diabetes, obesity, and physical inactivity.** Get screened to find out if you're at risk. To start, take the quiz on page 92. If you are at risk, work with your doctor to decide what actions you should take to reduce your risk.

DON'T SMOKE OR BREATHE TOBACCO SMOKE

Smoking or breathing tobacco smoke is the single greatest cause of preventable death among African Americans in the United States. Smoking makes blood vessels in the body stiff, greatly increasing your risk of cardiovascular disease and stroke. The good news is that when you do stop smoking—no matter how long or how much you've smoked—your risk of heart disease and stroke drops rapidly.

If you don't smoke, don't start. If you do smoke, stop now! **You have the power to quit.** Ask your doctor to suggest a smoking cessation program that will work for you.

American Heart Association® | American Stroke Association®

POWER TO END STROKE SM

You are the Power

WATCH YOUR BLOOD PRESSURE

High blood pressure (hypertension) is often called the silent killer because it has no symptoms. It affects nearly 43 percent of adult non-Hispanic black men and nearly 47 percent of women. Compared to whites, African Americans are more likely to have high blood pressure, develop it earlier in life, and have more severe cases. Hypertension is a major health problem in the African American community.

Have your blood pressure checked at least once every two years— more often if you have a family history of high blood pressure, stroke, or heart attack. In between visits to your doctor, you can also check your blood pressure at your local drugstore. The first number (systolic pressure) measures the force of blood in your arteries when your heart beats. The second number (diastolic pressure) is the force while your heart rests between beats. Compare your results with the chart below to see if you're at risk. If your readings are in the prehypertension or high categories, work with your doctor to lower your blood pressure.

Blood Pressure	Normal	Prehypertension	High
Systolic (mm Hg)	Less than 120	120 to 139	140 or higher
Diastolic (mm Hg)	Less than 80	80 to 89	90 or higher

KNOW YOUR BLOOD CHOLESTEROL LEVELS

Cholesterol is a fatlike substance produced by your liver. Cholesterol is also present in foods from animals (especially egg yolks, meat, poultry, seafood, and whole and 2 percent dairy products). Excess cholesterol can form plaque on the inner wall of your arteries, making it harder for your heart to circulate blood. Plaque can break open and cause blood clots. If a clot blocks an artery that feeds the brain, it causes a stroke. If it blocks an artery that feeds the heart, it causes a heart attack.

Among non-Hispanic blacks age 20 and older, nearly 45 percent of men and about 42 percent of women have total blood cholesterol levels of 200 mg/dL or higher. Are you one of them? **Get a simple blood test to find out if your blood cholesterol level is desirable, is borderline-high, or puts you at high risk of developing heart disease and stroke** (see the chart below). Contact your local American Heart Association to find out about free or low-cost screenings in your community.

Talk to your doctor about managing high blood cholesterol. Eating a healthful diet and being more physically active are good ways to start. If your cholesterol stays high, you may need medication to help reduce your risk. Be sure to take medication as prescribed, and talk to your doctor before you stop taking it.

Cholesterol Level (mg/dL)	Desirable (low risk)	Borderline-High Risk	High Risk
Total cholesterol	Less than 200	200 to 239	240 or higher
LDL ("bad") cholesterol	Less than 130*	130 to 159	160 or higher
HDL ("good") cholesterol	40 or higher for men; 50 or higher for women**		Less than 40 for men; less than 50 for women

*People who have had an ischemic stroke or heart attack (or are at risk for having one) may be advised by their doctor to keep their LDL level below 100, or if they're at very high risk, below 70 mg/dL.

**The higher, the better—an HDL level of 60 mg/dL and above is considered protective against heart disease.

MONITOR FOR DIABETES

Most of the food we eat turns into glucose, or sugar, for our bodies to use for energy. The hormone insulin helps glucose enter the cells of the body. When you have diabetes, your body doesn't make enough insulin or can't use its own insulin as well as it should, or both. This results in increased blood levels of glucose.

Diabetes is very common in the African American community, but many people don't even know they have it. Not knowing you have diabetes can lead to devastating health problems. **Have your glucose (blood sugar) levels checked regularly, especially if you have a family history of diabetes.** People with diabetes often also have high blood pressure and high blood cholesterol and are overweight, further increasing their risk for heart disease and stroke. Overweight or obesity is a major cause of diabetes. Losing weight can help stop or reverse the development of diabetes.

A random glucose test (nonfasting) reading of 185 or more or a fasting test reading of 126 or more, measured on at least two occasions, indicates that you may have diabetes. A fasting test reading of 100 to 125 indicates a condition called prediabetes. If your glucose level falls in either category, consult your doctor to learn how to monitor and prevent or manage diabetes. Prediabetes can cause health problems also. This condition is referred to as insulin resistance.

AIM FOR A HEALTHY WEIGHT

Obesity is a major concern for all Americans, including African Americans. You have a much higher risk of heart disease and stroke if you're overweight or obese, even if you have no other risk factors. Excess body fat—especially at your waist—raises blood pressure and blood cholesterol levels and increases your risk of developing diabetes.

You often can decrease your risk of heart disease and stroke by losing as little as 10 to 20 pounds. Establish a sensible eating and physical activity plan that will help you reach and maintain a healthy weight. Avoid fad diets and promotions that promise you will lose weight quickly. You don't gain weight overnight, so don't expect to lose it that way and keep it off for the long term. Obesity is not an appearance issue; it's a health issue. Whether you like the way you look or not, you owe it to yourself to develop a healthy lifestyle.

BE PHYSICALLY ACTIVE

It's well known that being physically active improves your cardiovascular fitness, but you may not realize that consistent inactivity actually increases your risk for heart disease and stroke. Physical activity can be as simple as walking briskly around your neighborhood or at your local school track.

Aim for at least 30 minutes of moderate physical activity on 5 or more days of the week. For example, you could spend 30 minutes of moderate physical activity on 5 days of the week or 20 minutes of vigorous activity on 3 days, or a combination of both to reach your goal. Being physically active can help you prevent or control high blood pressure, high blood cholesterol, diabetes, and obesity and overweight. Exercise can also help you reduce stress levels, give you more energy, and improve your self-image. Choose an activity that you enjoy, set reasonable short- and long-term goals, and remember to reward yourself along the way as you achieve your goals.

LEARN THE WARNING SIGNS AND TAKE THE PLEDGE

Learn to recognize the warning signs of stroke, listed below. Acting quickly when these signs occur can mean the difference between survival and disability or death. Share this information with your loved ones to show you care.

JOIN THE MOVEMENT!

Show your commitment: Take the pledge. Then copy this page and post it where you will be reminded that you have the power to end stroke.

- -

I'm real. I'm strong. I'm proud. But I'm at risk for stroke.

The American Stroke Association is ready to talk to me about what matters—to me.

They can meet me where I am—to make positive lifestyle changes.

They can make a positive impact—on me and my legacy.

So I pledge…

To not just survive—but thrive. I will learn how to live stronger and longer—for me, my family, and my community. I will join the movement to prevent and overcome stroke.

I will call 9-1-1 immediately if I or someone I know experiences these signs of stroke:

- **Sudden numbness or weakness of the face, arm, or leg, especially on one side of the body**
- **Sudden confusion or trouble speaking or understanding**
- **Sudden trouble seeing in one or both eyes**
- **Sudden trouble walking, dizziness, or loss of balance or coordination**
- **Sudden severe headache with no known cause**

Signature _____ Date _____

Call **1-888-4-STROKE** or visit **StrokeAssociation.org/power** for more information.

KNOW YOUR RISKS

You don't have to become a statistic! You have the power to reduce your risk of heart disease and stroke. The quiz that follows will help you see where you need to focus your efforts. Then work with your doctor to prevent, reduce, or control as many risk factors as you can.

✔ Check all that apply to you. If you check two or more, please see your doctor for a complete assessment of your risk.

AGE

☐ You are a man over 45 or a woman over 55 years old.

FAMILY HISTORY

☐ You have a close blood relative who had a heart attack or stroke before age 55 (if father or brother) or before age 65 (if mother or sister).

MEDICAL HISTORY

☐ You have coronary artery disease or you have had a heart attack.

☐ You have had a stroke.

☐ You have an abnormal heartbeat.

TOBACCO SMOKE

☐ You smoke or you live or work with people who smoke every day.

BLOOD PRESSURE

☐ Your blood pressure is 140/90 mm Hg or higher, or you've been told that your blood pressure is too high.

☐ You don't know what your blood pressure is.

TOTAL CHOLESTEROL AND HDL CHOLESTEROL

☐ Your total cholesterol level is 240 mg/dL or higher.

☐ Your HDL ("good") cholesterol level is less than 40 mg/dL if you're a man or less than 50 mg/dL if you're a woman.

☐ You don't know your total cholesterol or HDL levels.

PHYSICAL INACTIVITY

☐ You don't accumulate at least 30 minutes of moderate physical activity on 5 or more days of the week.

EXCESS BODY WEIGHT

☐ You are 20 pounds or more overweight.

DIABETES

☐ You have diabetes or take medicine to control your blood sugar.